SUCCESS AUTHENTICALLY

UNLOCK EXCITEMENT, PURPOSE, AND JOY AT WORK

ALLY BUBB

To your success!

Ally

Published by Work Authentically

All rights reserved.

No part of this book may be reproduced in any form or by any electronic or mechanical means, including information storage and retrieval systems, without written permission from the author, except for the use of brief quotations in a book review.

The material in this publication is of the nature of general comment only and does not represent professional advice. The author and publisher disclaim all responsibility for any liability, loss, or risk that may be associated with the application of any of the contents of this book.

ISBN 978-1-952078-02-6 (e-book)
ISBN 978-1-952078-03-3 (paperback)

Book formatting by Wolf Mountain Publishing

CONTENTS

Resources 1
Introduction 5
1. Misery 11
2. What do you want to be when you grow up? 19
3. What Is Success, Then? 25
4. The Success Authentically Formula 33
5. Who? 41
6. What? 55
7. How? 67
8. Why? 73
9. Where? 81
10. When? 95
11. Who? Part 2 105
12. Putting It All Together 111

Thank You and Free Gift 117
Acknowledgments 119
About the Author 121
Books by Ally Bubb 123

RESOURCES

Throughout this book, I mention other books, links, and additional resources. All of it can be found at:

WorkAuthentically.com

You don't have to worry about trying to remember links or the names of anything mentioned in this book; it's all a click away when you need it. Relax and focus on taking the right positive action for you.

To all the wonderful people still trying to figure out what they want to be when they grow up.

AND

To the many brilliant accountants out there doing amazing work every day.

INTRODUCTION

"Some of these questions don't have finite answers, but the questions themselves are important. Don't stop asking, and don't let anybody tell you the questions aren't worth it. They are."

– Madeleine L'Engle

Are you feeling bored and unfulfilled at work? Or maybe you'd describe it as completely miserable? If you are, you're not alone. It's a fact of work life for the majority of American workers and the statistics are bleaker when you look at workers globally.

What if I told you there was a better way? That there is a formula that you can use to unlock excitement, purpose, even joy at work. Depending on how long you've been suffering at your only-going-for-the-paycheck, soul-sucking job, you'd be skeptical. Maybe you're ready to call shenanigans now and move on.

Who could blame you? I know all about the dark side

of corporate America. The extra hours, the always on expectations, and the ever-increasing responsibilities without an ever-increasing salary. And that's in the good jobs! You have every right to be cynical. Trust me, I was. Except there's that tiny part of you deep inside that desperately hopes what I'm saying is true. I know how badly you want to believe, because I was once barely clinging to that hope as I slogged my way through work, days blending into weeks, months, and years.

Where do we go from here? We start by throwing out everything we thought we knew about success. If we want to achieve a different result, we need to be willing to take different action. If you genuinely want to unlock excitement, purpose, and joy, be open to the possibility in this moment. The questions that follow are going to help us forge a brand-new path. As with everything in life, the seemingly unrelated are often interconnected in ways we can't begin to comprehend.

Do you hate reading the news today? Do you find it depressing? Or maybe you think it's filled with gossip about allegedly famous people? Say what you will about the state of journalism at present. It's over the top. It's click-bait. It's nothing but doomsday proclamations. Maybe some of that is true, but to be fair, we've all played our part in making it so by only clicking on the absurd, over-the-top, click-baity, doomsday stories. Regardless, there's at least one thing that journalism got right.

Remember your 5th grade teacher? Mine was Mrs. Chynoweth and she was amazing! She was the most interesting teacher I had in elementary school. She wore those small plastic combs to keep the sides of her hair held back

INTRODUCTION

and she swapped out the color based on her outfit (yes it was the 80s!). She encouraged us to do interesting art and creative writing and try new things (for me it was learning calligraphy). She loved husky dog racing and got the entire class interested in the Iditarod. Mrs. Chynoweth, in addition to being an awesome teacher, is the one who introduced me to how to do better research.

Are you a parent to kids of any age? I have two wonderful, spirited children and guiding them toward adulthood has been one of the best and most challenging things to ever happen to me. Kids are naturally curious about the world around them. They explore, wonder at, experiment, and test the limits of everything simply to expand their understanding.

How do they do it? Well, it's a lot like researching a topic to write a great paper. It's a lot like the approach that journalists use to get to the heart of a great story. And of course, kids aren't thinking about any of that as they try to make sense of the world. They're doing what comes naturally to anyone who honestly, truly wants to learn more.

Any guesses on what all three of these have in common? They ask questions. Not just one question, a whole bunch!

"What questions?", you may be wondering (which is an excellent question to ask!). Maybe you can recall them from your elementary school experience. Maybe you remember them fondly from your journalism school days (before you had to get that soul-sucking corporate accounting job to pay the bills). It's the 5 W's, which is a bit of a misnomer, since there's actually 6 key questions that don't all start with W, but that is a far less catchy way

7

of describing it, so some call it 5W1H or 6 W's (allegedly because how has a w in it). Regardless of the way you want to refer to it, those questions are:
Who?
What?
When?
Where?
Why?
How?

And did you notice that every paragraph in this section started with a question? What a fascinating observation you've made (or perhaps an exciting discovery)! Questions are the building blocks for a great article or research paper or understanding the world. Questions can be a lot of fun when you're getting to know someone. Questions can help bring order and meaning when you're learning something new. I love a good question that makes you stop and really think.

But you know what's even more powerful than the questions? It's our own authentic answers to them. As a coach, I frequently ask clients questions and although the questions are often the same, the answers are dramatically different from person to person. We can talk about something as simple as what you want to eat for dinner or something as complex as what legacy you want to leave behind after you're gone and your answers to those questions will be different than my answers.

Why is that? It's because we have different personalities, strengths, weaknesses, interests, hobbies, life experiences, biases, relationships, and taste in music to name just a few reasons. All of these things and more are inputs our brains use to develop answers to questions. And since every single human on earth is unique, that means every single human could come up with a slightly (or dramatically!) different answer to any given question.

What does all this have to do with success? When we lack the answers to the six simple questions in the context of our careers, things can go terribly awry...

1

MISERY

"I'm no longer quite sure what the question is, but I do know that the answer is Yes."
– Leonard Bernstein

A GOOD JOB

From the time I can remember, there was an expectation that my brother and I go to college and get "good jobs". Graduating from high school was the starting point, not the finish line that had been set in our family. I don't remember ever defining what a "good job" was, other than knowing it was one where you got paid regularly for doing work and that it could only be secured through a college diploma. As a child, I never had an answer for the ridiculous question that adults love to ask of children, specifically, "What do you want to be when you grow up?" (I will save up my rant on why that question is fundamentally flawed for another time.) Despite not really knowing what I wanted to do with my life, I knew the next step was going to college.

My original major in college was in Business Administration, specifically Accounting. That felt like a great major that would allow me to get a good job and therefore have a good life. I mean, who doesn't want a good life?!?! That's a thing!

I'm not entirely sure how I even landed on accounting – maybe it was mentioned on a commercial or shown as a possible job in a tv show or maybe I closed my eyes and pointed a pencil at the course catalog page and it landed on accounting. Regardless of how I picked it, I made a plan to become a successful accounting superstar.

I was excited to get started and made sure to take accounting classes during my freshman year. I can't tell you how glad I am to have done that. It helped to clarify a few things for me after only two accounting classes: 1. Accounting was horrible and boring! (no offense to those who actually enjoy accounting) and 2. I couldn't imagine a worse fate than spending the next 40 years doing work related to accounting.

The clarity was fantastic as it kept me from wasting more money on a degree that I would despise. Ironically, the clarity also created a ton of uncertainty. I didn't know what else to do. I had no backup plan. You see, I wanted to be graduated in 4 years or less and on to the fun world of earning a living, so I'd already mapped out my classes for the next 3 years. As a result, I found myself in quite the quandary.

I ran-walked in a full-blown panic to my friendly academic advisor, who was one of my favorite people on campus, to let him know that not only was my graduating-in-4-years plan in serious jeopardy, but that I would no longer be one of those successful, gainfully employed people with a great job.

It turns out (and I don't know if you know this because I certainly didn't at the time) most colleges, including mine, offered more than just accounting for a major. Really! So we talked through several options of majors and minors that seemed to be more in line with my interests and skills and I set out to begin testing them out the very next quarter* (at that time, my college operated on quarters rather than semesters). First up on my list was to try my hand at the exciting, new-ish field of computing since it seemed interesting and definitely had potential for one of those "good jobs".

My first computer science class (C++ in case you're wondering) was pretty fun and it didn't make me miserable like accounting, so I never really explored anything else on my list. I simply updated my graduate-in-four-years plan with new courses and moved forward without thinking too hard. I sometimes wonder how differently things would have turned out if I had considered other possibilities.

Through a combination of good grades and good timing (graduating in 2000 when every company needed a website, database, and a whole lot of other computer-related things) I had my choice from several "good jobs" after graduation. Alright! Mission accomplished! I did it! Wait... what did I get myself into? I promised you some misery after all.

THE BEGINNING (AND THE END)

My first job was in a small Information Technology (IT) department for a large company in the manufacturing industry. I found the work to be boring and tedious and ended up leaving that job within the year. My next job I enjoyed more – it was in the financial services industry and had a much larger IT department. I loved the people I worked with, but there were many elements about my job that I didn't enjoy, including the very slow, very hierarchical culture of the company and my day-to-day tasks. I opted to stay in financial services at various companies for the rest of my 20 years in the corporate world, holding various roles and titles.

Some jobs I truly enjoyed and was disappointed when the time came to move on for any of the usual reasons (team was restructured, change in company strategy, company went out of business entirely – THAT one was exciting!). I won't bore you with the details of most of my jobs, but I do want to share one because I think it underscores several key points.

I had a great job. It checked all the boxes: reasonable pay, decent benefits, and flexible hours. It was challenging work, but I had a lot of awesome co-workers who I liked working with. And yet, something wasn't quite right...

It was 4 o'clock in the morning on a weekday and my alarm was ringing. The first sensation I became aware of as I awoke was how tired I felt. It had become progressively harder to wake up each morning and I assumed that I was a little overworked or perhaps on the verge of a cold. I made a mental note to look for a nutritional supplement to help with energy and kept going about my daily routine. I continued that routine, but never felt like I fully recovered from whatever it was.

You may be thinking that waking up at 4am on any day is a horrible, miserable, experience, but for me, it's awesome! I'm an unapologetic morning person. I LOVE waking up early! The simple fact that something so core to my being was no longer functioning as it had should have been a red flag for me. But sometimes we miss out on obvious clues.

Truth be told, I was continuing to feel worse. I started to have unexplainable dizzy spells. The doctors ran all the tests and each one came back normal (which was a relief!). The doctors didn't really have an explanation to my symptoms and instead I got a shrug as they asked, "Are you under a lot of stress at work?" I was under what I believed to be a normal amount of stress, so I didn't think much of it. At least at first.

A few months later, around 5 o'clock in the morning on a weekday (because the 4 o'clock hour had become impossible!), the first sensation I would feel each day as my alarm went off was a pain deep in the pit of my stomach. I didn't fully realize it at the time, or maybe I didn't want to acknowledge it, but it was dread. Absolute dread at the thought of going to work and doing the tasks I knew were necessary for success. I kept hoping it would get better. Maybe if I could suck it up and keep at it for another day/week/month the feeling to go away. It didn't. The pain intensified and I was miserable.

By this time, I had been to doctors for multiple health issues. Low back pain that couldn't be alleviated. The dizzy spells that had no explanation. The chronic exhaustion permeating all aspects of my life and making it difficult to do anything. As a person who has always been reasonably healthy and who didn't have any chronic conditions, I was scared. Something was very wrong with me, but each test kept coming back "normal". It was a relief not to be diagnosed with a terrifying or terminal disease, but it was also a struggle to understand why I felt so horrible if everything was "normal".

A few months passed, where I continued to have this pervasive sense of dread. The stress had reached a point where I wasn't able to fall asleep or stay asleep and I was up all hours of the night battling anxiety. One particular morning, I awoke with the dread, got ready as usual, and left the house to drive to work. I was driving on some lightly traveled country roads – the kind where you may not always come to a full stop at the stop sign because there's never any traffic at 5:30 am – and I could see another car approaching the t-intersection that I was about to drive through. The driver of the car didn't see me and opted for the less than full stop option.

By this point, the front of my car was well into the intersection and the other driver had to hit their brakes hard (lock them up style!) to keep from crashing into my driver's side door. Inches away from the other car, staring at how close I'd come to a potentially life-altering accident, I had a shocking realization.

I wasn't happy or grateful or even relieved. No injuries, no insurance claims, no car repairs needed and I had no sense of the good fortune that had been handed to me.

You know what I did feel, though? I was disappointed.

That makes no sense! Why would I be disappointed? I should be overjoyed that we can both go about our days with no catastrophe. Right? Except... since I wasn't in a car accident, I still had to go to work.

I want to stop for a second to let that sink in. Ok. Now let me state it as clearly as I can. *I would rather be in a car accident than go to work.* Yikes. THAT was the day I knew I needed to leave my "great job".

THAT DIDN'T GO WELL

I hope you are quicker than I was in the above example to recognize when you're not in a good job situation. For me, my subconscious mind and my body were sending me signals for months and I kept ignoring them. Why? Because on paper, it WAS a great job.

So, what was the problem then? Unfortunately, it wasn't a great job for me. I was spending all my time on energy-draining tasks that I didn't enjoy and it was slowly crushing my soul. Excitement, purpose, and joy were so far removed from my daily experience that I wasn't even sure they existed anymore.

It's not always about logic or pay or benefits or hours. You need to do meaningful work that you enjoy where you can be your authentic self with all your strengths and unique attributes.

Yes, we all have bad days. There are always going to be unenjoyable tasks, but you shouldn't be waking up feeling dread. That's not how a job should make you feel. Stop rationalizing it and listen to the signals your body is giving you. And if you've moved beyond dread and into the hoping-for-a-car-accident-so-you-don't-have-to-go-to-work phase, it's well past time to take action!

For me, the issue came down to my authentic self. And more accurately, the fact that I had deprioritized and ignored her completely for years. I honestly didn't even recognize myself anymore. For me, that was the scariest part of all. Because I hadn't been paying attention to what work I might really enjoy, or where I derived my energy, or how to best leverage my strengths and talents in service of things I cared about, I was lost. I had no ideas and no clear path.

At the end of the day, I walked away from a six-figure salary and a job title for one of the most marketable roles in my industry, with absolutely no plan or direction. I had a lot of fear. I had a lot of pressure to make sure my family was still able to cover the basics of food, clothing, and shelter. I had a lot of naysayers giving me "advice" to stick it out.

It wasn't easy to leave, but it had become impossible to stay.

The only thing propelling me forward was a vague sense that there had to be something more and I was determined to figure it out.

2

WHAT DO YOU WANT TO BE WHEN YOU GROW UP?

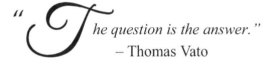

"*The question is the answer.*"
— Thomas Vato

STUPID QUESTIONS LEAD TO STUPID ANSWERS

Remember earlier when I promised you my rant related to this question? Buckle up! Or don't. It's unlikely you'll get overly jostled as I share it. But nevertheless, you've been officially warned!

I find the way that we talk with children about the world of work troubling. We start by asking 5-year-olds what they want to be when they grow up, as if they should have any clue about the world of work. I mean really.

It's a limiting question. It implies there's only one thing each of us can do, which is completely false. You and I and everyone else can be successful at an almost infinite number of endeavors.

This question is the source of angst and frustration for many people. One that for many of us is hard to answer because we simply don't know. It's even harder to answer in the 21st century, since many of the jobs the 5-year-olds of today will hold don't even exist yet (which doesn't stop grownups from badgering them about what they want to be when they are older)!

Even if we could see into the future to know what possible jobs are coming, most people aren't born knowing what work they want to do. For many of us, it's a long series of trials and errors before we land on something that suits us (and that's if we're one of the lucky ones that has the freedom to explore career options rather than being forced to gut out a job over decades simply to sustain ourselves and our families!).

We go on to tell kids stories like, you have to get good grades in order to have any chance of getting into a good college to get that mythical perfect job you're supposed to have known since you were 5.

Kids experience a ton of anxiety and stress trying to outperform or keep up with their peers academically, striving for ever higher grades and completing more advanced placement tests. By the time many young people get into college, they're already exhausted and burned out and the career adventure is just beginning!

Now they spend years in college, often incurring significant debt, to become the thing they thought they wanted to be when they were 5. Or maybe to become the thing they thought someone else wanted them to be. Or maybe to become the thing they thought would sound impressive when they introduced themselves at parties.

Or maybe to become the thing a parent said they had to be if they wanted to have their college paid by said parent. Or maybe to become the thing that will pay them so much money, they'll never need to rely on anyone else again. And finally, graduation! We get to go to work for the next 40 or more years! Huzzah! It always seems like fun when the first few paychecks come rolling in, and then our reality begins to set in.

For many of us, when we finally start doing the work we've been trained to do, we discover that we don't really love it. So, we try a different job. Then another one. Then another. But nothing seems quite right. We feel like a failure for not loving the thing we were supposed to be. We feel like a fraud for continuing to show up every day for a job that we don't enjoy. And worst of all, we feel ashamed for being the only ones that couldn't figure out what we wanted to be when we grow up!

Anybody else ready to vomit in their mouths and give up? Or is that just me?

OVERLY DRAMATIC GASP YOU MEAN TO TELL ME YOU DON'T KNOW?

People seem shocked if you don't have an easy answer to the basic question of "What do you want to be?". As I share in my book, *Change Authentically: A Guide to Transform Your Job and Life Through Positive Action* (Bubb 2020):

"It implies a single job, a single type of work and boxes people into thinking there's only one thing out there for them. It's a fundamentally flawed question, one that creates more misery than we realize for anyone who has multiple answers or worse yet, no answer!"

We end up with a vague sense that we've failed the answer to some kind of life test, forgetting that "What do you want to be when you grow up?" was really just a way for a grown up to interact with a child when they don't know what else to say to them.

Let me be the first to say it's OK if you don't know what you want to be.

Statistically speaking, I've made it halfway through my career and life (though tomorrow is promised to no one) without an answer for this fundamentally flawed question. And I'm OK with that. In fact, I'm more than OK with it!

I've stopped believing that this is a helpful or useful question. I don't ask it of children or adults because I know the angst and uncertainty it creates.

Let's think back to that hypothetical scenario from the beginning of this chapter. We start by asking kids a flawed question, we tell kids stories to support that flawed question, and we send them off in search of grades and eventually a diploma to allow them to officially answer that flawed question.

At no point do we try to carry on a different and more productive conversation instead.

We don't stop to ask the critical questions that would help everyone much earlier on the path. Questions like: *What am I good at? What do I enjoy? What lights me up inside? How would I describe my best self? What problem do I want to solve? In what area of the world do I want live? What do I stand for and against? What legacy do I want to leave? What do I want my major contribution to be?*

The answers to these questions are dramatically different than the answer to "What do you want to be when you grow up?" They chart a different path. They lead us to entirely new and sometimes unexpected places. They help us start to surface our authenticity.

But most of us haven't been asked these questions by someone else and we definitely haven't asked ourselves.

The question becomes the answer. We need to start with better questions if we want a better outcome. We need to change the focus of the narrative to help people live into the best version of their most authentic self.

As David Whyte says far more beautifully than I ever could in his amazing book, *Crossing the Unknown Sea: Work as a Pilgrimage of Identity*, "To have even the least notion of what we want to do in life is an enormous step in and of itself, and it is silver, gold, the moon, and the stars to those who struggle for the merest glimmer of what they want or what they are suited to." (Whyte 2001)

Figuring out the least notion, as Whyte calls it, can sometimes take our entire lives! It isn't something that happens when you enter kindergarten. And it's not something that is static over the course of a lifetime either. Very few people finish in the same type of role/industry that they start.

Does anyone remember the start of the book with the dedication? In case you don't want to flip back, this book was dedicated to everyone who still has no idea what they want to be when they grow up. But I think we can all agree now that's grade-A malarkey. So instead, let's re-dedicate it as follows:

To everyone. Except that one jerk we all know who had their career figured out since the time they were 5. But they don't really count since they're the exception to the rule, rather than the rule. So, to everyone else.

3

WHAT IS SUCCESS, THEN?

"The tragic irony of life is that we so often achieve success or financial independence after the reason for which we sought it has passed."
– Ellen Glasgow

ONE PROBLEM

Remember that time when my whole life fell apart a few chapters ago? That was so not awesome! But it did provide some good lessons!

Although I had a "successful job", it was actually a terrible job for me.

Have you ever been so miserable in your job that you wished for a car crash so you wouldn't have to go to work? I know it's dramatic, but my work as a career coach has proven to me time and time again that I'm not the only one to ever feel that way.

I love how one of my clients described it so eloquently:

"If someone told me I could cut off a limb right now in exchange for never having to go back to work, I would do it in a heartbeat. Cutting off a limb would be far less painful than another day there."

Yikes.

If you've worked (or are working) a job that makes you feel even an ounce of what I've been describing, my heart goes out to you. That is extremely challenging to go through. If you haven't been on the receiving end of a good dose of organizational misery, consider yourself lucky. Here's what you're missing.

One of the best ways to explain it is to use an excerpt from one of my own journal entries, written not long after I quit that "successful job".

From society's point of view, I was a success story. I had worked my way up the corporate ladder to middle management before my 40th birthday. Six figure salary at a stable company, nice house in a safe neighborhood in the suburbs, a pension, a 401(k) match. I had it all. Except that I didn't. I was miserable. And not in a I had a bad day kind of way. Miserable at the very thought of going to work and doing what I was paid to do. Dreading each day as it approached. Exhausted by day's end; practically incapacitated by week's end.

So I quit. I wish that I had a spectacular story about how I told them all off and quit with an epic flourish so legendary that people will talk about it years from now. Except that I didn't. I'm not independently wealthy and I will need to work for money. And I live in a small market where everyone knows everyone, so burning bridges to the ground was not something I could do.

What I wasn't prepared for was the response from people. Because on paper it seemed as though I had it all. And everyone, though well-meaning wanted me to stay. To keep having it all. Even though I explained my abject misery. It was like how I felt about my life should be an afterthought. "I'm miserable," I'd say. And the well-meaning person would reply, "Yes, me too. Only 10 more years to go!"

That doesn't seem like the makings of a good life...

I've got 27 years before the government's official retirement age. And if I try to spend it miserable, I won't survive. I barely made it out alive as it is. So now people don't know what to say to me. It makes everyone else uncomfortable that I don't have a reasonable answer to the question of what will you do next. But for the first time ever, I'm putting my comfort and my interests ahead of society's expectations and all those well-meaning folks who want me to stay as miserable as they are. Ask yourself: What if there's something more for me to do in the world to make a living? To make a life? What would I do if I listened to myself instead of everyone else? What if I was brave enough to architect a life I actually want to live?

TWO WORDS

I was already starting to ask myself a lot of hard questions, some of which had never occurred to me to ask before. Chief among them, "What does success look like?" You see, I knew exactly what success looked like in the corporate world. I understood the people, the hierarchy, the roles and assignments, as well as how to navigate those things to continue to move up the corporate ladder. Technically, that's success. I was successful at work. I did great work and people seemed to like working with me. I knew the answers to the question "What does success look like?" at my corporate job.

However, the question changes dramatically with the addition of two words: for me. When I started to explore the question of "What does success look like <u>for me</u>?" I was initially at a loss for words. I had no idea, no real guesses, apart from some glib answer that people spout off when complaining about the job that's making them miserable. It was some vague notion of not having to work anymore and laying in a hammock in the shade. Beach optional.

Truth be told, I'd never spent much time thinking about the *for me* part of the question. It was an unnecessary input. I knew what I needed to do to become successful at work and I set about doing it. As you can imagine, I was grossly underprepared for the shocking realization that defining success for me was actually WAY more important than how any company defined it.

I read every book on purpose and meaning that I could get my hands on. I was desperate to find my calling. The thing I was made for. The one true work for me. And for 20 years, I felt like one of the cast-offs on the Island of Misfit Toys in the Claymation holiday classic. (Rudolph the Red-Nosed Reindeer 1964)

I didn't find purpose or meaning, partly because I lacked an understanding of my authentic self. It was disappointing, frustrating, maddening even sometimes. Where was my one job? Where was my calling?

I kept on reading the articles and books that were telling me I could find it in 3 easy steps. But it never materialized for me. I had lots of interests. I had a great set of skills and strengths I could deploy. If only I could find that secret, one thing that had eluded me my entire life.

Finally, I had to call shenanigans and malarkey. This conspiracy has gone on far too long.

I don't believe there is one job or one type of work for each of us. I know now I could take my strengths and talents and find lots of ways to deploy them meaningfully. I'd found a way to be successful as a telemarketer, a web developer, a waitress, a computer help desk person, a front desk clerk at a hotel, a project manager, a requirements analyst, a technology educator, a product manager, a team lead, a presenter, an IT leader, and plenty of other roles.

And that's true for every single person on this planet. We can all be successful in myriad ways.

I'll grant you that some individuals have managed to find work they truly enjoy that gives them meaning and challenge, pay and benefits, autonomy and the like, but according to Gallup surveys, that's less than 15% of the global population. (Clifton 2017) In an 80/20 world, finding your one true calling would be considered the exception to the rule, NOT the rule.

So, what to do when your purpose is as mysterious as how the flux capacitor makes time travel possible? The best approach is to do some more digging to discover or uncover your authentic self. Once I started to resurface the me that I had lost along the way, a funny thing happened. The best way I can describe it is a lack of resistance. Everything stopped being So. Unbelievably. Hard.

All of a sudden, things were simpler. I was still working hard and committed to quality work, but the obstacles in my path were cleared or were easier to get around than they had been in the past. The resistance I'd felt up to that point wasn't there.

It was a strange sensation to be sure.

In the past, I'd figured out how to be successful in lots of roles in lots of ways, but never as defined by me. For all my roles, it was a lot of work to assess the people, processes, and systems and the corresponding definition of success for any organization. It was challenging and stretched and grew me in different ways. But it was never satisfying or fulfilling. It felt much more like a check-the-box activity rather than anything remotely enjoyable. It was a path filled with friction.

When I started to move toward the "for me" part of the question "What does success look like?", the friction dissolved. It didn't magically make everything easy without any challenges, but it did remove a layer of resistance that I didn't even realize I'd been bumping up against my entire working life.

Defining success for me helped me move beyond the "one job for every person" fairy tale and into an exciting world of possibilities.

THREE DIMENSIONS

If you were to take all the thinking, advice, knowledge, wisdom, classes, videos, business books, memoirs, and stories of a friend of a friend regarding success, we could summarize them into only a few dimensions. This is

SUCCESS AUTHENTICALLY

because as much as we are unique humans and will value different types of success differently, they are still related to three key areas. At its core, we're all seeking success as a person, in work and life, and in the world.

Success as a person means that I'm living into the best version of myself. Most reasonable people don't dream of becoming an angry, stressed-out jerk, but that can be the version of themselves they are living into regularly based on circumstances. You've probably bumped into just such a person on the street, or in a cubicle at the office, or where you live! Those interactions are never fun, but it's a little easier when you remember that this poor person is failing miserably at living into the best version of themselves.

Success in work and life means doing those things that are important to me. At work, I'm engaged, challenged, and am sharing my strengths with my organization. In life, I'm doing those activities I care about that bring joy. Most people, myself included, struggle with this dimension as the overwhelming tsunami of must-do tasks and responsibilities wash over us on a daily basis. This dimension is not about finding balance. It's about carving out time for the things that are important TO US and then doing those things regularly.

Success in the world means that I'm participating in something meaningful. Most people long for this type of success. Particularly as we age, doing things that will create or solidify our legacy tend to become far more important to us. Often, people have achieved success in the other two dimensions and are finally ready (or finally have the free time) to dedicate themselves here. I, however, am a huge advocate of stitching this meaning into your present-day reality, rather than waiting for some far-off distant future that may or may not materialize.

If you want excitement, purpose, and joy at work, it's time to dive into how we go about creating the success we seek.

4

THE SUCCESS AUTHENTICALLY FORMULA

"We have to look, examine, investigate. We have to find what's really true, not just accept what someone else tells us."
– Sharon Salzberg

SUCCESS FORMULA

Does math make you nervous? Me too! Sometimes I wish I could remember all the great math stuff I had to learn back in school. It would probably be helpful. At a minimum, it would make me less sweaty when I encounter math outside the basic operations of addition, subtraction, multiplication, and division.

I was actually fairly good at math in my younger years. Through a series of interesting events, I ended up in an accelerated program starting in junior high where I was the youngest kid in my math classes, taking them with the upperclasspeople (Sidebar: I find it interesting that spell check recognizes upperclassmen as a word, but not upperclasspeople).

Even with taking advanced math courses, I've always had that nervous-sweating feeling about it. I think it was working in the abstract, rather than the real world that bothered me. The problems on the page seemed a million miles away from where I was. And traveling on a train going 65 mph while someone else traveled on a train in the opposite direction at 72 mph was not going to get me there.

I enjoyed learning math, but often wondered why I would ever need it or use it in the "real world". I know there are many brilliant people using math to solve our everyday problems, build algorithms for the software we use daily, and so much more. Those people simply aren't me.

In fact, I've managed to make my way through daily society without needing those complex word problems involving trains, binomial factors, or differential equations, so I'd argue that part of my brain IS better off remembering 90s music lyrics (good thing, since I've got an extensive catalog of lyrics trapped in my brain!).

So, for anyone else feeling sweaty at the prospect of doing math or calculating out a specific number, know that we're not going to spend our time doing that here. *collective sigh of relief!*

The formula is an expression of the factors that go into success for each of us, and can be used across the dimensions of self, work and life, and the world.

The Formula:
(Who + What) * How * Why * (Where + When)

. . .

Just by remembering our basic math and order of operations, you can see that WHO, WHAT, WHERE, and WHEN are additive. HOW and WHY are multipliers. To put it in the simplest non-math terms I can muster: Things that add up are more than what you would have with just one thing. Things that multiply get much bigger much faster.

Even if you chose to only focus your efforts on those items that are additive, you'd see greater success by combining them than by ignoring them. And if you spend time on the pieces of the formula that are multipliers, you just added rocket fuel to your success engine. Or maybe a Mr. Fusion to your Delorean, depending on how you like to travel. (Back to the Future 1985)

We are going to be talking primarily about how this formula applies to your career because, well, I'm a career coach! And because this is often the area of our lives where we struggle most with seeking and finding success. My clients frequently share with me that they struggle with getting aligned to true success within their careers.

I'll also share some examples along the way of how I've seen the formula at work in my own life on the path to become my best self and helping me live into my vision of a better world.

As we talked about, those three dimensions (self, work and life, world) encompass the ways that we stumble on what works and doesn't for each of us as we try to do better. Rather than continue on the throw-spaghetti-at-the-wall-and-see-what-sticks approach, the Success Authentically formula provides the structure we need to move past all the stuff that doesn't work, without being so prescriptive that it's limiting or forcing us to calculate a single number. Hopefully, we're all feeling less nervous and sweaty!

AUTHENTICALLY

As much as it's a structured formula, don't for a minute think it's static. The Success Authentically formula is infinitely customizable and will achieve a different result for every single person that applies it. You get to control all the variables, which is good since we all will want different results. What works for me may not work for you, and vice versa. That's why defining what success means to each of us is so critical.

Cooking is something I believe everyone should have a firm grasp of since we eat three times a day (at least!). Unlike decorating for a specific holiday which you do once a year, learning to cook will pay off huge dividends daily!

When I graduated from college and started living on my own, I found out that I wasn't a very good cook. I only really knew how to make macaroni and cheese, frozen pizza, and cold cereal. That lifestyle gets old fast, but you can't just snap your fingers and become a great cook. It takes time and practice.

One of the first times I realized this was when I was a volunteer in the Big Brothers Big Sisters program. My Little Sister and I had hung out doing fun activities and school activities, but I was super excited for the day when I was able to spend an afternoon with her baking. Truth be told, I'd never spent an afternoon baking all by myself

SUCCESS AUTHENTICALLY

before. I'd always had others helping me, whether my roommate in college or my parents.

I found an easy recipe for oatmeal raisin cookies and my Little and I got to work. The dough came together easily enough, which gave me a dose of unfounded confidence! I didn't know that you need to space cookies apart because they spread as they bake. We stacked the dough tightly on the pan, put them in the oven, set the timer, and then went back to chatting and having fun. I mean, we were two busy, young women who didn't have 10 minutes to spare standing around watching cookies bake!

When the timer rang, we had a tray of half cooked dough that more closely resembled bars. We were able to save a few corners for cookie bites and had to toss the rest since it was an undercooked, mushy disaster! My Little and I were disappointed at the result, but we had a good laugh about it and moved on.

Fast forward a few years and I got much better at cooking, mostly because I was doing it with some regularity. Add a few more years of experience and I got better still. Now, I'm able to whip up pretty much anything from scratch at any time I feel like it.

This doesn't mean that I'm a 5-star Michelin chef, however. I've found an approach that works for me. I refuse to spend time on overly fussy recipes (read: inefficient!) or on things that require me to dirty every pot and pan I own. It's not that I can't do those things; I prefer not to. I don't love washing dishes, so the fewer I use, the fewer I have to wash. I also have a young family that requires my time and attention, so I choose not to spend all day in the kitchen preparing one to-die-for dessert. If that's your thing, call me. I'm an expert dessert sampler!

Some of my friends love to bake, but don't love to cook meals. For others, it's the opposite. For some, they choose to eat out more frequently and cook less. I have no issue with any of those approaches because it works for them.

You can think of the Success Authentically formula more like a recipe that you would use to make an amazing dish. The recipe is the basic instructions and following the instructions blindly may not yield a delicious dinner. This is where your authentic self comes in. You get to modify the recipe based on personal preferences (I'd rather have Lacinato kale than purple kale), dietary needs (use gluten-free flour instead of wheat flour), and what you have on hand (we're out of shallots; substitute red onion instead).

In the same way, you get to modify the formula to achieve your own version of success based on personal preferences (willingness to work fewer hours for less total money to spend more time with family), needs (there's still a minimum dollar amount necessary to pay the mortgage), and what you have on hand (the skills/strengths/superpowers you bring to the organization).

If I were to give 100 chefs the same recipe, no two dishes would turn out exactly the same. The chefs would each infuse their own unique characteristics into the dish. They have different experiences and preferences that will guide them to tweak the recipe. Similarly, if I were to give 100 professionals the same Success Authentically formula, no two careers would turn out the same for the exact same reasons as the chefs. That's what makes cooking and building a career so exciting!

We will all start with the same information as building blocks toward our own version of success, but we will each approach it differently based on our unique style, approach, and way of being. Let's take a deeper look at those building blocks – the 6 W's.

5

WHO?

"What we know matters but who we are matters more."
– Brené Brown

IT'S NOT WHAT YOU KNOW...

Sometimes it's hard to see in advance how the relationships we build over time will turn out to help us in our success. There are relationships that you expect to provide help and support who sometimes let you down. There are relationships where you didn't think you were that close, and they surprise you with an amazing gift. There are relationships that come and go over time depending on our location, hobbies, interests, and life ages/stages.

We never know when and how the people in our lives will be there to help us avoid disaster, cheer us on, support us, or slap us across the face so we can snap out of it. But every time it happens in my life, I'm extremely grateful for them.

I'm a big believer in trying my hardest to be a decent human being, so I implore you not to build relationships simply on the basis of what you think you'll get out of them or how they'll help you. The folks that start with this approach often find themselves stranded and alone during the lowest points of their careers and lives. People can tell when you're using them or when you're doing all the taking and no giving in a relationship.

Let's save a lot of time and trouble at the outset and vow not to be the grouchy, friendless, classic Dickens character, Ebenezer Scrooge. Build real relationships from the start and you won't have to wake up on Christmas morning promising to change! (Dickens 1843)

Relationships and WHO we know factor greatly into our success. How many times have you heard the career adage, *"It's not what you know, it's who you know"*? If you're like most of us, you've probably heard this "advice" more times than you can count.

There are a few dangers in taking this saying at face value. First, people incorrectly assume that they need to know the "right people" to get the job. You can spend a lot of time and energy trying to find the folks you think might be the right people, but end up not being able to impact the hiring decision the way you'd thought. Second, people are quick to use the *"...it's who you know"* part of the saying as an excuse when they don't get a job. It's also an easy out for folks to not even try for a job sometimes because "it's all about who you know."

Implicit in the adage is the belief that WHAT you know

doesn't matter. It gives people a reason not to focus on delivering quality work. It also provides ample ground for excuses around not doing your work at all.

As with most pieces of conventional wisdom, there is some element of truth to the saying, but it's a harmful belief if left unexamined.

Don't get me wrong, WHO you know is important, but important in different ways than this adage suggests.

RELATIONSHIPS MATTER

I don't know about you, but I wasn't born into a family of CEO's. I didn't go to a fancy, private school (ever, actually!) with other well-connected children of CEO's. We didn't summer in the Hamptons or winter in Aspen (two places I've never been, in fact). I wasn't on a sports team with the child of anyone famous. When it came time to be hired for my first real-world job, the odds weren't on me getting it based on WHO I knew.

I worked hard in college to maintain a decent GPA while also working multiple odd jobs to scrape together enough money to pay for school and have a little cash left over for Friday and Saturday nights (and let's be honest, most Thursday nights too!). What kind of odd jobs? Waitressing. Front desk clerk at a hotel. Telemarketing on behalf of the university. Help desk person in the computer lab on campus. None was my dream job, though all had elements of things I enjoyed, at least sometimes. More importantly, they were the motivation I needed to keep moving toward my degree and that goal of a "good job." I knew that I wouldn't want to continue doing any of these as my "one true calling" for the rest of my life, so I needed to get a new job.

What's the best way to get a new job? Interview for one! At least, that's the best approach I'd come up with at that time, so I put all my spare time and energy into getting interviews.

Back in my college days (any sentence that starts this way makes you seem old, doesn't it?) it wasn't as simple as clicking on an "Apply Now" button to get an interview. The internet existed, yes, but people weren't using it to apply for jobs. Most web pages either had a visitor counter and some amount of flames or an under-construction graphic on them.

I needed to physically walk to the career center building on campus and see which companies would be coming to campus to interview. Then I'd have to sign up on a paper form in order to reserve a spot, if I met the minimum requirements. On my first visit, I signed up for a company that I thought would be fun to work at and that had a great reputation.

I went to the interview, wearing my one suit, expecting to be handed my offer letter by the end of the discussion, since I was a hard worker and fun to be around and a great employee at all my other jobs.

Needless to say, they were under impressed with me. With no pending job offer, I needed to up my game. I decided to expand my job search and sign up for more than just companies that might be fun or have a good reputation.

My new target company was Anyone-That-Would-Pay-Me-For-Work-Related-To-My-Degree-Program! And it turned out that my expanded search criteria significantly increased the number of companies I could talk to.

I had a dogged perseverance to keep on applying to potential jobs, regardless of how many no's I'd gotten (it was a lot!). I subjected myself to a grueling interview process with pretty much any company that would have me simply to ensure I had an entry-level job when I graduated.

Like any job search, it took time, effort, and some amount of good luck. The perseverance thing came in handy for sure, but there was more to it than that.

Remember that helpful academic advisor I mentioned earlier who helped me pivot when my initial plan of accounting thankfully did not work out? Let's call him Brad, shall we, since that was his name.

Brad was one of my go-to people on campus. I didn't have close relationships with many professors, but I regularly checked in with Brad. He helped me not just develop my plan to graduate in 4 years, but also had a lot of wisdom to provide around how to change the plan as interesting things happened (like when I didn't take quite enough Spanish for a minor, but did have enough for a certificate in International Business). He knew the university, the programs, and the people like the back of his hand. And most importantly, he was a positive, encouraging beacon of light whether I was struggling with a seemingly impossible class, stressed from final exam week, or I'd gotten what seemed like the millionth NO in my job search.

Brad knew my strengths and my goals. And when he got a call one week before school ended for the year from an alumnus that wanted to hire 4 summer interns, I was on Brad's short list of recommendations. Was I more skilled than anyone else at the university? Not really. I'd taken roughly the same classes in a similar order and didn't have a ton more knowledge than anyone else.

I didn't know the company nor was I familiar with a single person that worked there (I hadn't ever been to the city in which it was located!). They definitely didn't hire me based on WHO I knew there. And as a mid-college person with a large amount of enthusiasm and a relatively low degree of actual, real-world knowledge and a handful of relevant classes, they didn't necessarily hire me based on WHAT I knew either.

Why, then, did they hire me? Even with the full benefit of hindsight, I still marvel sometimes at my delightful bit of luck and good timing, quite honestly.

Brad was a person that I trusted. And it turns out he was great at building relationships, so he was a person a lot of people trusted. That trust translated into an implicit endorsement of my skills. And for the alumnus who would otherwise have to swim through a sea of paper resumes to try to find decent candidates, that was enough. The 4 of us on Brad's short list stood out to the hiring alumnus because a person they trusted suggested our names. We went through the interview process like everyone else, but it almost seemed like it was our job to lose rather than to win. When the interview revealed that we were indeed as qualified as anyone else regarding WHAT we knew, the decision became easy.

They hired all 4 of us for a summer internship.

What can we learn from this? As I mentioned, I didn't know anyone at the company that eventually hired me. For all the cynics that think you have to know the CEOs and give up before even trying when they don't, this proves that approach wrong. And Brad, though awesome, was not a Senior Vice President of the Such-and-Such for any company. For all those that think there are "right people" to network with, this proves that approach wrong.

Let's revise the adage into something more useful for people: You stand out based on WHO you know.

BE A GOOD HUMAN

I've held several jobs in customer service (although I'd argue we're all in the business of serving some customer, no matter what our official title is) and those jobs gave me the opportunity to see some of the best and worst behavior from people. I can tell a lot about your character just by watching how you interact with service people, whether it's waitstaff, hotel staff, or someone you talk to on the phone after you make it through all the automated prompts.

I know some people pride themselves on being able to yell at someone, demand to speak to the manager and then get some restitution for a perceived wrong. Don't be that person, Karen.

I'm not saying that you shouldn't ask for something in return if your hotel reservation is messed up or you're frustrated with how few airline miles you're accumulating on your credit card. I'm saying, don't be the person that yells about it. Because really, there are very few things in life worth yelling at someone else over.

It might feel good to vent and get your frustration off your chest when you're angry, but think about it from the other side. The person receiving your complaint has probably gotten a whole bunch of complaints over the course of a day or a shift. Yours isn't going to stand out to them. You're just another complaining customer in a sea of complaining customers.

You know what will stand out? Using your manners. Saying please and thank you. Speaking with kindness and respect. Talking to other humans as if they are a valued member of your team or family. Showing empathy and understanding. Acknowledging that the other person is doing the best that they can given the circumstances.

From small, annoying situations through stressful, crisis situations, when someone treats you well, you are more willing to help.

Think about your current job and the people you interact with regularly. Is there a person that often complains to you about something not working well (regardless of if it's something you are responsible for)? Do you look forward to those interactions? I'm guessing no. But what about the person who always has something nice to say, even on the most miserable project? I'm willing to bet a large sum of money that you are more likely to help the second person, rather than the first when the opportunity arises.

One of the many jobs that I held during college to scrounge up enough money to pay for said education was working at the front desk of a small hotel. Being a college kid, I often worked the shifts no one else wanted, like holidays, evenings, and weekends. I was glad to have a job that paid me and it was interesting work. I enjoyed taking reservations on the phone using the green screen terminal, handing out pool towels, and answering questions on local cuisine.

As with any job, I have plenty of stories of interesting things happening there. The list includes helping 3 senior-aged women get their rental car started one chilly morning, busting up an after-hours pool party, and consoling devastated people the morning that Princess Diana died in an accident (and the morning newspapers had gone to print before she passed away). As many stories as I remember, many more have been lost to time and the finicky nature of memory.

There is one story, however, that stands out vividly for me.

It was a Saturday night like any other and the hotel was nearly always full on the weekends. This was no exception. Every single room was sold out. There were people in town to visit loved ones, participate in tourist activities, and even to enjoy a local hockey tournament.

There were several groups of people that were staying at the hotel together so they could eat dinner at the restaurant, have their kids play in the pool, and enjoy the fun of going from room to room. As you might imagine, hijinks ensued (why else would I be telling this story?!?).

Around 9pm, a young boy decided to create a little more fun and excitement for everyone. He pulled the fire alarm to see what would happen. The alarm went off, exactly as it should have, and everyone evacuated the building until the fire department arrived and determined it was a false alarm.

Everything went back to normal and the hotel quieted

down for the evening around 11pm. Until the fire alarm went off again. Apparently, the alarm had been pulled with such vigor the first time that some internal parts were damaged, and those loose parts triggered the alarm to go off again. And again. And again. Throughout the course of the evening and into the wee hours of the morning, everyone's sleep was interrupted multiple times by the erroneous alarm.

I wasn't working the front desk when the fire department showed up. Or the night shift when the broken alarm continued to sound. Nope. I was out with my friends enjoying a Saturday night (as one does in college!). Instead, I found out about the incident a few minutes before 7am when my shift to run breakfast and check out the entire hotel was about to begin.

I enjoyed the autonomy provided by my front desk clerk job. I had plenty of freedom to rearrange the desk to flow efficiently for me, to move the phone holder from the right shoulder to the left one, and to interact with guests and staff alike. However, one of my responsibilities as front desk clerk was non-negotiable. I was required to ask every single person at checkout, "How was your stay?" And I was dreading asking each person because I KNEW how their stay was. It was annoying, disrupted, and frustrating.

I dutifully got an earful from nearly all of the guests that morning. They let me know just how angry and frustrated they were. Some let me know they wouldn't be staying with us again. I was authorized to offer reduced room rates to help smooth things over if requested, but even with that, most people were short on sleep and resultingly, short on patience with me.

No judgment here! I am a terrible human and make far

less decent and reasonable decisions when I haven't had enough sleep, so I completely get it.

After several hours of angry complaints and disgruntled check outs, I was feeling pretty bad. None of what happened had been caused by me, but I was bearing the brunt of the bad feelings everyone had as a result of the fire alarm experience.

That is until the most wonderful, decent, and reasonable human came to the desk. I'm sure she could sense in my defeated body language the fact that I was bracing for her answer when I asked, "And how was your stay?" She surprised me and told me it had been unlike any she'd had in recent memory. She more or less laughed it off and didn't see any need to pile on to the stack of complaints I'd received that day.

Interesting. Her statement was equally true for all of the guests that morning, but no one else had chosen to respond by leaving the anger and frustration out of it. Everyone could have said their stay was unlike any in recent memory.

The next guest in line overheard what that woman said and I believe that she was influenced by the first kind person. When I asked the next guest, "How was your stay?" She acknowledged how difficult the morning must have been for me. "It has been," I replied, "but I understand where they're coming from." She said a few more encouraging words to me, left her keys on the counter and continued on her way.

Remember, I was authorized to offer people discounts on their room only if they asked to help smooth the many ruffled feathers, but it wasn't something I was to bring up otherwise. However, I was so appreciative of the kindness that both of those guests showed me that I gladly offered them the discount, even though they didn't ask! One turned it down and the other accepted, but I made the choice to show my appreciation to both of them, even though I technically should not have.

Beyond those two people, there was one other person that was particularly kind to me that morning. It was the mother of the child who pulled the alarm. She was embarrassed, contrite, and extremely apologetic, especially after eating her complimentary continental breakfast across from the front desk and having a front row seat to the anger and frustration directed at me. I appreciated her apology, but no, I did not offer that family the discount!

The rest of the morning was a blur of checkouts and complaints and the usual goings-on of a busy morning at a hotel. And yet, those three kind and decent people stand out in my memory more than 20 years later.

Today, I am so grateful to those three guests for showing me understanding during a challenging time. It was a powerful lesson to learn and it's one that I try to bring into my interactions, no matter how frustrated I am. I may not succeed every time, but I absolutely try. Kindness and respect are the minimum I can offer to another human, especially one whose job it is to interact with customers. Plus, you never know who will offer up a discount, room upgrade, free dessert, or other perk to people they enjoy working with!

Now, as a parent of kids right around the age of the boy who set this whole adventure off all those years ago, I can only imagine what a challenging night and morning that family must have had. I hope they're able to laugh about it the way I can when I think about it today!

As Bruce Wolf writes in his awesome management book, *How to Manage A Team Like a Decent and Reasonable Human Being: You Can Become A Great Leader Just By Not Being a D!ck*:

"Forget about the latest fad that your Big 4 consultants are trying to sell your executives. It's the same one they're selling your competitors and it's not going to do you any good anyways. I know that reimagining the framework, bending the curve, and torqueing the outcomes, or whatever nonsense buzzword catchphrase is in season this month sounds amazing and necessary, but I promise you, it pales in comparison to being a decent and reasonable human being." (Wolf 2020)

Relationships matter. How you treat people matters. Regardless of level, rank, position, hierarchy, or any other superimposed reporting structure, be a good human. We all like to help nice people… and will often go out of our way to do the opposite for anyone that's been a jerk to us!

6

WHAT?

"The purpose of life is not to be happy. It is to be useful, to be honorable, to be compassionate, to have it make some difference that you have lived and lived well."

– Ralph Waldo Emerson

BUSY IS THE NEW FINE

We spend most of our time on WHAT, and although it's important, it's by no means the most important part of the Success Authentically formula.

At work, the majority of our time is sucked away by WHAT we do, or WHAT our boss has delegated to us to do, or WHAT our team needs our help with, or WHAT is the latest shiny-object or business-altering strategy as determined by executive leadership.

We have precious little time and energy to get above the daily tidal wave of tasks. If we do, just when we're starting to make a little headway, another wave comes crashing down on us dragging us back to the WHAT through the force of the undertow.

Overwork has become so common that most people now consider a ridiculous amount of work to just be work. The stress and overwhelm that come with too much work are now deemed normal. We answer the question of, "How are you doing?" not with how we're actually feeling, but with a simple statement of the fact that we have way too much WHAT: "Busy! How are you?"

I'd be willing to bet that if I called the CEO of the place where you work and asked if they pay you to be busy, I'd get a resounding no (possibly right after they say, "You're calling about who?!?!" and quickly look you up in the org chart!). The importance of having you do WHAT you do every day is not in how busy it keeps you.

When we talk about WHAT we do, it's really about the value we bring to an organization. When you shift your thinking to focusing on value, the tyranny of the urgent falls away and you can create focus for yourself on WHAT will most move the needle on any given day, week, month or year.

Does the value come in sending an email? Usually not. But there's probably a handful of emails that make the difference. Emails where you're clarifying expectations are invaluable to the person that needs clarity. Emails that provide a good experience for someone that is waiting for information from you. Emails that can remove obstacles for your team are a godsend for the folks that have been stuck and churning.

But most of the emails we send are unnecessary or

unimportant. *Yes, I'll attend that meeting (even though there's no agenda and it's probably not required). Yes, I got your email (but if it was so critically important that I see it and respond immediately, why did you send it by email? There are far better methods for instant response, including talking to each other!). Sure, I'll weigh in on that topic that we're still going to discuss in a meeting later this week (but likely won't make a decision or move forward at the meeting!).*

When you start to focus on value, it's a lot easier to wade through the sea of WHAT to find what matters. A great way to filter through all the WHATs is to keep asking the question, "Will this matter in a year?" If not, maybe it's not the best use of your time now to get you where you want to go.

I acknowledge that there are certain instances where it may feel you have no choice but to do whatever is asked of you, no matter how absurd or time-wasting. Believe me, I've been there and that's no fun. I'd also suggest that we often don't try to differentiate between what matters and what is being asked of us right now. Sometimes it's easier to nod our heads and do the thing rather than ruffle any feathers. I'd encourage everyone to push back and ask the question for anything that is deemed urgent, must-do, or immediate response needed. Those words are usually a cover for something else going on in an organization. And it sure helps the team and boss look busy, doesn't it?

Remember when we spent time exploring, *"It's not what you know, it's who you know"*? Great, because it just happened a chapter ago!

Let's further revise the saying into something more

useful for people: You stand out based on WHO you know; you still get hired based on WHAT you know.

A related corollary to this adage: If you don't deliver, you will be relieved of your duties in time. It likely won't be immediate, but it is an eventuality. Anyone who's seen this play out not over weeks and months but over years, knows it can seem endless and be a huge drag on team morale as everyone waits for it to come. It does happen though, so don't lose sight of the WHAT any more than the WHO.

HI, I'M BORING

For most of us, the idea of introducing ourselves to someone else for the first time makes us very uncomfortable. The discomfort can range from mild, jittery butterflies in our stomach all the way to throw-up-in-the-parking-lot-before-we-go-inside panic.

Why are we so afraid of this activity? Simply because it is awkward. And being awkward is considered bad. Awkward feels so unnatural, unless you're like me and used to being awkward everywhere! Then, it feels like every other day, but it doesn't necessarily feel good.

So, we dread introducing ourselves and through this dread, give up a great opportunity to have an interesting conversation with another human being. And yet, we know the question of "What do you do?" is coming our way. It's extremely likely to be the second question after your name.

But we let the dread stop us. You see, it's the way we're conditioned to introduce ourselves. We immediately say WHAT we do in the simplest terms possible to get it over with. Worse yet, we tend to keep the WHAT in the format of our job titles. Talk about boring AND awkward!

"Hello! What do you do?"
"I'm a Project Manager 2. What do you do?"
"I'm a Systems Analyst 3. Great to meet you!"

Gross. Did anyone besides me throw up in their mouth a little after reading that? Exactly! Introducing ourselves like this is vomit-inducing (which is all the worse if you were the one puking in the parking lot from nervousness before we even got started!).

I probably don't need to mention this since the odds are high that you're a human (if not, welcome non-human!), but this type of awkward exchange is not typically the way humans talk to each other. Why in the world would we take something as awkward as introducing ourselves and make it exponentially more difficult by reciting our invented-by-HR job title to each other?

I'm going to suggest something radical, that can transform the awkwardness around introducing yourself into something enjoyable, maybe even fun.

Don't say your job title.

Earth-shattering advice, I know. I want to remind you there are no rules around how you choose to answer the question of "What do you do?" (although I'd love to offer up that it be true, since most human interaction thrives on trust). Basically, throw away everything you thought you knew about networking and spouting off your job title and instead think about WHAT you do.

Go beyond your knee-jerk reaction of selling something or installing something or fixing something. WHAT do you really do? Think about the value that people get from the work you do.

Do you make life easier for a group of people? Do you make something more efficient? Safer or more reliable? Do you connect or provide a missing piece to others? Do you identify priorities? Do you coach and develop people?

There are probably lots of ways you provide value and you'll see them if you list them out. So, if you're working from a giant list of things, which of those things should you select to say WHAT you do? The first consideration is WHO you'll be meeting. If the audience is a room full of accountants, you will want a WHAT that is interesting to them. They may not care about the innovation work you're doing, but might be fascinated with how you drive strategy through fiscal responsibility.

The next consideration you can use to filter the list is impact. Think about all the WHATs you do and determine where you're having the biggest impact. Not only will that be an interesting WHAT to share with someone else as an introduction, it'll also be a fun thing for you to talk about (see, I told you we could make this fun!). People can tell when we're genuinely having fun and when we're faking it and most people will choose to keep talking with someone they find interesting or fun.

Even if you hate your job (and chances are good that you do!) introducing yourself this way gives you an option to talk about the one or two things you actually enjoy, rather than the soul-sucking array of tasks associated with your job title.

I share two key pieces of my own WHAT when I introduce myself: "I educate and empower people…" It makes it clear right away where I focus my energy as well as the value I bring. People specifically hire me to do exactly that; teach them what they need to know and encourage and support them to put that knowledge into action.

Is saying I'm a career coach or a speaker bad or the wrong thing to say? No. It's a true statement and definitely fits within the socially acceptable bounds of listing out my job description. But it doesn't start any meaningful conversation when I introduce myself that way.

When I flip my introduction to WHAT I do, when I share that I educate and empower people, almost everyone I meet has a question around that. The most common response is, "Wow! Tell me more about that!" Isn't that the impression you want to leave with someone when you meet for the first time?

You have the choice to make your WHAT interesting and impactful, as well as the permission to never say your job title as an introduction again!

THE ONLY CONSTANT IS CHANGE

As people, we're in a state of constant change. The change is so gradual we don't notice it from day to day, but it's happening. We continue to refine our preferences, interests, hobbies, habits, beliefs, and more over the course of our lives.

Have you ever bumped into someone you haven't seen in years? The changes in them are much more pronounced and easily visible to you. Or maybe you've had that terrifying experience of waking up and not recognizing the person you see staring back from the mirror.

The small changes add up over time until they can't be ignored, whether they are changes in others or changes in ourselves. I'm thrilled by that news because it means I can keep growing into a better version of myself! I shudder to think how my life would be different if I was stuck with some of my former mental models, habits, or beliefs that no longer (and maybe never did!) serve me. WHO I am is not fixed and static; it is growing and changing and with any luck, growing and changing in a direction that I have intentionally set.

Didn't we already spend some time talking about WHO we are? Great of you to notice and remember! It's relevant to the discussion on WHAT we do because most of us derive some or all of our identity from our jobs. This is one of the reasons people often struggle with any other sort of career transition. When people ask us, "What do you do?" (and they WILL ask us, right after our names as we explored already!), we don't say, "I work in the field of education." Nope. We say, "I AM a teacher." It's part of our identity; it's WHO we are.

When I left my corporate job without a plan (not typically the recommended option!), I had absolutely no idea how to introduce myself to new people that I met. If I'm not Ally who does software development at a well-known company, then who in the world am I?

I had a hilarious moment in a group setting where the majority of the group knew each other, but we were asked to introduce ourselves to two new people who had never met the group before. I had only recently left my corporate job and had not thought at all about what to say to the question of "What do you do?" in part because I'd never imagined not doing what I had previously done.

The panic started to rise within me as each person in the group spoke and shared what they did. Time stood still as my brain went blank, my blood pressure skyrocketed, and I started spontaneously sweating. I mumbled through an explanation that was weak, unclear, and extremely uncomfortable. Whew! Not my best work, but at least the pain was over and someone else was talking about what they do.

It was at that exact moment that a dear friend leaned over and whispered, "Well that was super awkward! You're going to want to work on that."

Ouch.

But she was completely right, both on my awkwardness and the fact that I needed to get my head around WHO I am now that I'm not the person I thought I was. WHAT do I really do?

Just as we are constantly growing and changing as people, the same is true of our careers. Sometimes, it's an imperceptible career change like taking on a new responsibility to go with your existing ones. But sometimes, it's a full transition from one thing into something else completely different.

There are lots of career transitions and like any transition, navigating one can be a challenging journey.

There is the transition from length of time you work. When you transition from full-time to part-time work or vice versa, it's a whole new schedule and approach, even if you keep doing the exact same job at a different capacity. That schedule change can be the source of challenge and adjustment for weeks or months. Some people find that they never fully get used to the change and end up switching back if it doesn't work for them.

There is the transition from your classification as a worker. This could be going from an employee to contractor or from a small business owner/entrepreneur to working for a large corporation. Sometimes, the transition is a change in the way we approach work. Going from a steady corporate paycheck to freelancing or running your own business is a dramatic change, and one that should be considered in light of all the data, factoring in both risk and reward, in order to decide.

Then there is the transition from working to not working. This can be a joyous time, perhaps in the case of parental leave or retirement (both of which can also be an awful time!). It can be a time of panic and crisis in the case of an unexpected layoff. When our identity is wrapped up in our work and we suddenly stop doing work, it can be a real blow to our self-esteem. Many people struggle with depression during these types of transitions, and if you even remotely suspect that could be you, seek out professional help immediately because depression is nothing to mess around with.

Though we are growing and changing all the time, we may not notice it until we enter a period of transition. The nature of the newness we experience can be enough to jolt us awake and make us take stock of everything we thought we knew. That re-evaluation can bring the changes within us and outside of us to the forefront.

In addition, transitions are inherently tough to navigate simply because they involve a lot of change. For most of us, change is really hard. We often fight against the change, even when we are transitioning into something we have wanted/dreamed about for a long time. So, imagine how much more complex the emotions are when transitioning to something we don't want. Fear is a major issue.

As I share in my book, *You Got This!: Move Beyond Fear to Make Change Happen!* (Bubb 2020):

"I've coached clients through monumental changes and helped and supported friends as they make amazing things happen at work and in life. The simple difference between anyone that can successfully make change happen and those that can't comes down to what they do when faced with fear."

Unfortunately, many of us are unprepared for the fear that awaits us as we enter a period of transition.

Add in the complexity of ego and believing that we are what we do and it can get ugly. The feeling of being lost and misunderstood, especially by ourselves, can be almost too much to bear.

Don't go giving up now! Here's WHAT we do (see what I did there?).

WHAT we do isn't sending emails, though we lose hours of our life doing that.

WHAT we do isn't our job description, though we introduce ourselves that way.

WHAT we do isn't our identity, though our ego is completely wrapped up in it.

At its core, WHAT encompasses your value and impact. WHAT is also shaped dramatically by your HOW and your WHY.

7

HOW?

"Because our gifts carry us out into the world and make us participants in life, the uncovering of them is one of the most important tasks confronting any one of us."
— Elizabeth O'Connor

A UNIQUE APPROACH

We've established that we're all unique, special individuals (just like everyone else!) and the distinctiveness we each embody is incredibly important in our approach.

The way you do something is unique to you, even though you've likely been trained to do it a certain way. This applies whether you're following a recipe, taking a project from start to finish, singing in a choir, or any other activity. Sometimes we say that someone "made it their own" when we see a particularly interesting or unique approach on display.

That uniqueness means that even if you and I were hired for the exact same job description, we would approach our work in different ways. In fact, even if we scored the same on a personality or strengths assessment, we would STILL approach our work in different ways. Wait a minute! Didn't that fancy test help to generalize information about people like me and then create groups of people that are similar? It did, but those results are only part of the story.

This is often where corporations struggle when they try to staff roles assuming that any person with skillset X will deliver exactly the same way. We are wonderfully diverse humans, not robotic automatons! It's actually a challenge to try to emulate someone else's approach (yup, I've tried!) and to find any level of success in doing so.

In a world of infinite snowflake combinations of skills, backgrounds, and personality traits, the math is against us being able to plug people (and don't you dare call them resources!) into roles based on skillset to achieve the same results. It simply doesn't work that way and more often than not, everyone involved gets frustrated when they are put into a situation like that. No one can meet the expectation of doing it just like someone else did/does.

It would stand to reason then, that identifying your HOW is an important piece of knowing what you're great at. You can't tell others about the awesome work you're doing if you don't know yourself, can you?

Many of us in the corporate world will frequently find ourselves in a role that is similar to someone else. We might have the exact same job title even! Sometimes, there will be a clear differentiation of how the roles are different, like different departments or different customer segments. Sometimes, there will be no such clarity and people will wonder why we need a team of 5 people doing the same job.

Regardless of where you see yourself in that mix of organizational hierarchy, this is actually great news because it makes it much easier for you to home in on your HOW.

All you need to do is watch your peers.

You'll see HOW they approach their work that is different than HOW you approach yours. Note that we aren't passing judgment on which way is best (at least I'm not! You do you!). We are simply noticing the differences.

As you pay attention, you'll begin to see the ways that you approach your work that is unlike your peers. When you notice it, write it down! Start to capture a list so that you can refine it as you go. Most of the time, it's harder to notice HOW we do something because it's on autopilot for us. We just do it. We can't imagine approaching our work in any other way, which makes it both unremarkable to our own eyes and hidden in plain sight.

We need to intentionally stop and take notice of our HOW because it's a multiplier in the Success Authentically formula. It's also a source of personal excitement and fulfillment as you deliver something in a way that no one else can!

WHAT DO YOU DO AGAIN?

Remember when we spent all that time talking about WHAT you do? Let's revisit it for a minute.

We know that in an introduction-type setting, we absolutely will be asked, "WHAT do you do?" and now we're prepared for that question. We want people to understand the value we bring. We also know that we are free to answer that question in any way that is authentic to us and our story, rather than with our job description. Already, you have an advantage with a more interesting introduction to share with someone else.

When we think about our work, leaving those annoying HR-invented job titles behind, it can often be summarized into simple terms. Some people solve problems. Some people fix things. Some people build new stuff. Some people imagine and plan. Some people design.

For me, I'm an improver. I make stuff better than it was before. It doesn't matter if it's really terrible stuff or really awesome stuff, I can find a way to improve upon it. I can't even fully explain the steps my brain takes as it identifies the areas to improve or the steps that can be modified. It happens without me being fully aware of the process. But it happens. Sometimes, it's immediate, like during continental breakfast at a hotel where I am compelled to build out a new layout to eliminate the traffic jam at the toaster. Sometimes, it's a complex, multi-dimensional challenge that takes several weeks or months for the improvement to materialize. This is HOW I do what I do.

Unfortunately for my family, I also can't turn off my approach when I leave work for the day. There is almost nothing that escapes my watchful improver gaze except my spouse's belongings! I try hard not to interfere there unless my services are specifically requested which creates much more harmony in our home. An important lesson I learned early in marriage: There's nothing worse than being told you're doing something incorrectly! So, I do my best to keep my brilliant improver ideas to myself in that regard. As much joy as improving gives me, not everything or everyone is looking for it!

As I was saying, in our home and family life, we try new schedules, new furniture layouts, new plants in the yard, new organization for kids toys, new twists on meals, and a whole lot more on the regular. We have two geriatric cats for whom these changes are met most often with open disgust. If you've never suffered the baleful gaze of a cat who has been inconvenienced, consider yourself extremely lucky!

Angry cats aside, for the most part my family accepts and appreciates this in-built need within me. They humor me and allow me to tinker. I am beyond grateful that I am able to live into one of my strengths daily as so many of my career coaching clients are not in roles where that's the case.

Just as identifying your HOW is an important piece of knowing what you're great at, identifying your HOW is an important piece of your introduction in order to super-charge it.

But HOW can we use this in our introduction (see what I did there?)?

Going back to the idea that even if WHAT we do is exactly the same, including job title and personality assessments, HOW we do it will be different. So, let's celebrate the HOW and share that with others.

I am improver at heart and strive to make things better. As part of my introduction, I include HOW I do what I do: "…to take positive action…." HOW do I do my work? I help others improve their careers. I help people take positive action to fix the things that aren't working for them! That's one of my favorite things to do!

I love getting updates from clients after they've made the switch to a new job and hearing how dramatically different their life is now. The misery is gone; they actually enjoy their work (it's more than possible, it's probable!). Like a caterpillar becoming a butterfly, the transformation is incredible.

Your HOW is a superpower. It's that unique approach you have that helps you do what you do like no one else can. It's as natural as breathing (we often don't even know we're doing it!). The key is to harness that strength and apply it to something that matters to you (your WHY!) to achieve extraordinary results.

8

WHY?

"When something is important enough, you do it even if the odds are not in your favor."
– Elon Musk

NAH-GONNA WORK HERE ANYMORE

In the same way that HOW will be different (even if we follow the same process) for each of us, our WHY also varies from person to person. WHY we do something is incredibly important. WHY is often the difference between champions, medal-winners, award-winners, and everyone else.

Why would that be the case (see what I did there?)?

More often than not, we already know what we need to do to make anything happen in work and life. If we aren't sure of the steps we need to take, all we have to do is ask Alexa to have Siri Google it. So, it stands to reason we should all be the fittest, smartest, best versions of ourselves, right? Well it doesn't work that way because of WHY.

WHY is the reason we do or don't do things.

And when our WHY is aligned to our career, it multiplies our success. Of course, when our WHY isn't aligned, it leads to mediocre results at best and more likely active disengagement in our workplaces.

My first job after I graduated from college was for a well-known, global appliance manufacturer. Their WHY was to make life easier for people through top quality appliances. I mean, I think it was. Or it could have been something else entirely. I wasn't especially interested in the world of appliances, it turned out!

As a young person new to the world of adulting, I didn't have an appreciation for appliances and the various features they offered. If a stove could make a frozen pizza and macaroni and cheese from a box, it had all the features (and more!) that I needed! I also didn't see the need to have a ton of appliances in every home, because restaurants!

The reason I had taken the job at the appliance company was not because the idea of cooking and baking made my heart beat faster. It was not the idea of an improved home life for people everywhere. It was because it was my only job offer to do a specific type of work that I was interested in. And because they were going to pay me for it, of course!

I'd had other offers to do work at companies that I might have felt more aligned to, but it was work I was far less interested in doing. So, it seemed like a great choice to go with the work that was most aligned with my interests and skillset. Unfortunately for me, the job I had been offered was no longer available by the time I started at the company and I was re-deployed into a role that I'm sure my manager thought I would enjoy. And so, I became the database admin for the fledgling website.

It was a combination of no interest in the products and no interest in the day-to-day work that helped me quickly make up my mind to move on. I felt meh everyday when my alarm went off and I had to drag myself out of bed to go to work. My only joy was Friday afternoons as I counted down the minutes until I could leave work and meet up with my friends. I was truly workin' for the weekend!

I did the minimum of what was required of me and not much else, which isn't the way I like to approach my work, but I simply couldn't get excited about any aspect of it.

Their WHY and my WHY were completely and utterly misaligned and I was doing a disservice to myself and the company if I stayed there feeling as disengaged as I did. You'll be glad to know that before I left, I used my employee discount to get a high-quality blender because I did understand the importance of a good margarita!

Besides the blender, my parting gift was a real-world example of a company mission and specific work that didn't excite me; I knew to pay better attention to those pieces going forward in my career.

0-MINUTE ABS

We've all heard the promises from programs telling us we can be fit in a few minutes a day. Things like 10-minute abs or a 20-minute, fat-blasting, total-body workout make for great marketing, but they don't necessarily help me to look like any of the images of the fitness models they use to promote them. If you want to be in great shape, you need to work out for more than 20 minutes a day.

I've always been in awe of people who have the dedication to do that higher level of exercise. They are the ones that go to the gym after working a long day. They are out there before most people wake up in the morning, pushing their own limits. They are mindful of everything they eat to best fuel their bodies. They are committed to the work they need to put in so they can be the most fit version of themselves.

I've done comparatively short stints of working out to meet a specific goal but have never been compelled to take it further.

In high school, I did track & field, cheerleading, and volleyball. Please don't be overly impressed; I went to a small enough school where if you expressed interest, you nearly always made the team. I would commit to doing whatever workout and exercise was needed during the timeframe of each sport, but as soon as one season was over, I was done with the program.

That all changed when I attended a volleyball camp one summer led by women on a college volleyball team. I learned all sorts of new training and drills designed to help me be better at volleyball. I was beyond exhausted and sore after the week-long camp, but I was energized to improve. My dad helped me to set up a program where I was doing all of the training and drills every single week.

I was amazed at the difference it made. I got stronger. I got faster. I got better.

Sidebar: maybe this is why professional athletes train

year-round so they can gain and keep an edge! Who knew?!?!

I was super excited to start the volleyball season after all my training. I couldn't wait to play other teams and put my new skills to use. Our team had never been a powerhouse, so I wasn't expecting to win a state title or anything, but I thought we'd have a great season.

Instead, our season started off a little rough. We were out of practice, a little sloppy, and we ended up losing our first game. And our second. I was hopeful that the next team we played we would fare better. We didn't. Surely the odds only increased that we would win the next time after each loss, right? Well, the math didn't support me on that one. We never won a single game. We were winless for the entire season.

I saw the benefit of putting in the work to do the training; I also saw that it wasn't enough to carry a team to victory. And so, I retired from volleyball.

I had a WHY (be the best version of me on the court!) but that didn't help my team and it sure wasn't enough to keep me on a grueling training program long-term.

In college, we talk about the Freshman Fifteen. It's an acknowledgment that most people gain weight their first year of college for a variety of reasons: eating mostly pizza when given the freedom to do what you want, staying up late and snacking, drinking lots of… err…umm… "soda", you get the idea.

My brother (a year older than me in school) was convinced I'd be the latest freshman to succumb to the extra 15 pounds and he challenged me to a bet. I love a good challenge (and winning money!), so I jumped at the chance. My WHY was a powerful one: prove someone else wrong!

I started going to the gym multiple times a week and it was effective at maintaining my weight. Over time, however, I really began to enjoy going to the gym. My roommate and I would work out together, we'd blast music we both enjoyed, and we'd laugh and have fun. My WHY shifted from prove my brother wrong to stay healthy.

WHY IS FOR TENACITY

After I graduated college and got into the work world, I needed a new challenge. Entry-level work is usually far from exciting and mine was no exception. I'd been running for fitness for a while, but there are only so many 5k and 10k races you can do before it stops being exciting. So, I got the big idea to run a marathon. Yup. Running 26.2 miles sounded like a good idea to me. I must have been REALLY bored and unfulfilled at work! My WHY was to push my body further than I ever had and see if I have what it takes to finish a marathon. It was a personal test of endurance that I thought would be fun. And yes, I'm aware that my version of fun is dramatically different than many others'!

I found a book with a marathon training plan for beginners and got started. The first thing I needed to do was sign up for a race. My commitment to training skyrocketed once I was accepted. Fun fact: There are actually so many people that want to run marathons that many races have to turn people away! Can you even imagine?

With the official date locked in, all I had to do was follow the weekly training plan from the book to get ready.

The race was easy and one of the most fun mornings I've ever spent, despite horrible weather at the start and having to run 26.2 miles to get to the end. The hard part wasn't the race itself; it was every single day before the race.

I had to decide to get out of bed and run before work. I had to give up a large chunk of time on a weekend for a long run and the recovery that my body needed afterward. I had to ensure I was eating in a way to fuel my body for running. I had to overcome mental and physical obstacles weekly. I had to do the work. There was no short-cut I could take that would deliver the results I wanted.

As I said, the race was comparatively easy. It was the training and prep work that was challenging. But my WHY sustained me for 5 months so I could enjoy race day to the fullest. My WHY got me up on cold mornings and hot mornings and everything in between. My WHY helped me push past my physical limits and mental barriers as I inched ever closer to running 26 miles consecutively.

My WHY was to push the boundaries of my athletic abilities and finish a marathon. Once it was over, I had no real reason to keep running. I wasn't doing it for cardiovascular fitness or weight management or pure love of running. I was doing it to finish a marathon. Once I crossed the line, my WHY stopped being compelling enough to get me out of bed in the mornings.

Similarly, thinking it would be cool to have defined arms has not been a compelling enough why in over 40 years to make me take the action and get to the gym to make that wish a reality. The WHY doesn't move me.

It's not aligned to my values. It doesn't help me live

into my vision for my best self. It doesn't even get me to pass up a slice of cake when it's handed out at a wedding!

The most powerful way to supercharge your success is a WHY that will keep you chasing it even when the journey is difficult (it will be) and obstacles arise (they will) and success itself feels a million miles away. A short-term WHY might help you hit a short-term goal, but it's not going to be the thing that moves you forward over the course of your career. We're potentially talking about 40 to 60 years of working (depending on when you choose to start and stop), so a short-term WHY isn't going to cut it. We need something that moves us forward, even after we achieve big goals and aspirations.

WHY do I do what I do? If you'll recall, I've been down the road of misery to the point of wishing for a car crash to not have to go to work. It ain't fun. And I want to help people who are heading down that road, who are suffering, who need to talk to someone who gets it.

But my WHY goes deeper than that because I've also seen the other side of misery. I know what it's like to experience pure joy doing work as well. It transforms not only the person doing the work, but the workplace, the lives of others around them, and ripples out into the world.

That's WHY I do what I do. I want to transform the world through others finding joy, purpose, and meaning. I've seen personally and professionally what a difference it makes for individuals, families, workplaces, and the world when people are filled with joy instead of misery.

9

WHERE?

"I stopped worrying about the start. The end is what's important."
– Usain Bolt

ADVANCING YOUR WHAT

There are definitely right places to be and wrong places to be. In a scary movie, you know the wrong place to go is the basement. And you for sure don't want to run upstairs if you're being chased! That is the absolute wrong place to be if you want to make it to the end of the movie alive!

It's the same reason why venturing down a dark alley at night is ill-advised. That's the wrong place to be.

Hanging out with the cool kids in high school (or at any age, really) and getting caught toilet papering someone's house? Wrong place. Especially if someone calls the cops. At a minimum, I hear they will make you clean it up (and I promise you that job is no fun!).

There are plenty of wrong places, many of which are clearly obvious, and some of which are only obvious in hindsight. You're probably thinking of a wrong place you've been in your life too.

So, what are the right places? The right places are places that can help you advance your WHAT, HOW and WHY.

If you want to do any type of work, one of the best ways to learn more and get connected with others in the space is to hang out with people who do the kind of work you want to do! It sounds obvious, but many of us miss this important point if we get too focused on WHAT we want to do, without giving consideration to the rest of the Success Authentically formula.

There's a reason Alexander Hamilton wanted to be in "the room where it happens". (Miranda 2015) It was a place WHERE important discussions were being had, a place WHERE key decisions were being made. It was the difference between success or not for Hamilton, and it's the difference for us too.

Often, our WHERE grows organically over time as we make our ways through our careers. We know WHERE the movers and shakers are in our industry. We know which companies have a reputation for being the best. This is one of the most overlooked aspects of the formula for many of my clients. Hanging out with others who do the sort of work you want to do becomes critically important if you're a new graduate or a career-changer.

You need to start putting yourself WHERE the work happens in order to learn the room where it happens in the context of your new career. It's about being open and asking as many questions as you can to anyone that is willing to answer them so you can start to find out.

You may not have the benefit of knowing many people in the industry and you will want to spend time in the places they are in. That could mean a particular coffee shop near the office. It could mean inviting people to virtual coffee. It could mean talking with someone with absolutely no coffee involved (but why?!?!). The point here is that you want to start learning about the people doing the work in the places where the work is being done.

Remember that time I quit my corporate job without a plan? Again, not the recommended approach, but more often than not, we start with where we're at under far less than ideal circumstances.

Since I began the journey of building a business from the ground up, I've reached out to many people who are experts on all sorts of different topics from marketing, to book publishing, to entrepreneurship, to other career coaches. Not everyone has had time to help me or share their knowledge, but the vast majority have pointed me in directions to find out WHERE I need to be for particular topics.

Sometimes the WHERE is joining a particular group that aligns with my goals. Sometimes it's sharing my knowledge with others by speaking, presenting, or teaching. Sometimes it's being on a virtual call or webinar to hear wisdom from people who have walked the path before me. Sometimes it's meeting with my mastermind group to share ideas and support each other when things are working, and especially when they're not.

As I became more skilled in the technology field, I got

promoted, as most people do. It was exciting to have new responsibilities and those came with the opportunity to learn a whole new WHAT.

I started off my first project manager role doing what I'd always done before: figuring it out as I went along. It worked alright for me and I eventually became competent in WHAT I needed to do to be successful.

Thankfully, I was WHERE I needed to be to improve.

I was on a team that had many project managers and each of us was assigned multiple projects of varying sizes to manage. As we chatted in the hallway one day, we began to notice that we all had a different approach (shocking, I know).

And so it came to pass that we started meeting regularly to talk about what was and wasn't working with our projects. It allowed us to share ideas and eventually draft a set of best practices for each of us to follow. It instantly gave each of us access to the experiences everyone had had and it soon became clear that even though there were new projects and problems, we had seen it or done it before in some form or fashion.

By virtue of being WHERE people were doing WHAT I was doing, studying those best practices, and seeking out more information on the discipline of project management, I went from being competent at my WHAT to being one of the best.

Getting better at your WHAT happens slowly over time, but you can fast track it based on WHERE you are.

When you're learning something new (and even when you're a seasoned veteran!) there is something magic about being in the proverbial room where it happens. It sets you up for success to advance your WHAT in ways you can't begin to imagine!

You may have some very clear ideas on WHERE you need to be to advance your WHAT. Awesome! Turn those ideas into action and see WHERE it leads you! You also may have no idea WHERE to start (see what I did there?). Don't despair! Instead, start asking anyone you can to point you in a direction.

You may be surprised to discover how much knowledge people are willing to share when someone approaches them and is genuinely curious about the work they do. And that knowledge will be invaluable to you on your journey as you seek out the best WHEREs to make it happen.

ADVANCING YOUR HOW

The best coach I've had the opportunity to know was not a person with a formal coach job title. She was a manager at one of the companies I worked at early in my technology career. Let me tell you about Lois.

Lois was and is one of the most encouraging people I've ever met. She has a way of making people feel great simply by being herself and saying what she's thinking, because by and large, what she's thinking is encouraging stuff!

Whenever I had a meeting with her, had lunch with her, or saw her in the hallway, I always left the interaction feeling more positive and uplifted. Lois always highlighted something good about me and reminded me to keep doing what I do. In a stressful, harried workplace, she spread joy and encouragement instead.

Giving that feeling to others now is one of my primary goals in my coaching work. I know how helpful it can be because I've experienced it! I also know from my times of misery that encouragement is often the missing piece when you're in a space where you're questioning if your co-workers understand the value you bring.

Lois had a way of talking about the work that I did that made it sound so much more impressive than when I talked about it. As my manager, I would often tell her about something I was working on, challenges and all, and she would listen and ask questions. The magic would happen when she would restate what we'd just discussed, but she managed to highlight areas of my approach in a different way than I had talked about them.

I didn't fully grasp what was happening at the time, but Lois was helping me to articulate my HOW.

She was pointing out how my approach differed from my peers. She was pointing out the ways my approach was adding value by helping to solve problems or deliver something important to our clients. She was highlighting aspects of my approach that were so automatic for me, my brain didn't even register them as anything special.

At that point in my career, I didn't understand my approach to doing work was unique to me. I hadn't seen enough or done enough to appreciate that fact. Lois helped me put language around the work I was doing and to articulate my HOW in a way that was both understandable and compelling to others.

One of the saddest days at work for me was the day she retired. I hadn't formally reported to her for the better part of a decade by this time, but I truly missed talking with her on a regular basis. Some of my best days had been the days we'd accidentally bump into each other and chat for a few minutes. Her encouragement was like a booster shot to help keep me going during challenging times at work!

I'm grateful to being in the right place where someone else saw my value and helped me see it too. I'm grateful for learning a way to communicate my HOW that resonates with others. Most of all, I'm grateful to have been coached by someone who was an expert at encouraging others, giving me the basis for my own coaching approach all these years later.

Being in a place where you have a coach/mentor/leader to guide you is <u>always</u> one of the right places. It shapes your career in profound ways. If you're not in a place like that right now, seek someone like that out in your professional life. It will make a dramatic difference.

ADVANCING YOUR WHY

I have a love of the natural world. It's been a part of me since I was a small child. I hated seeing litter on the ground. I couldn't understand why any person would throw garbage wherever they felt like and make a mess of our beautiful planet. In fact, it bothered me so much I would pick up the garbage. As an added bonus for me, I lived in a state with a 10-cent refund on aluminum cans, so picking up a can was basically like finding a dime on the ground! Whenever I found one, I'd pedal my bike as fast as my legs would carry me to the local grocery store to cash in on my riches.

Unfortunately for me, I also had a love of candy (nearly

as great as my love of the natural world) and my 10-cent piece of litter translated into 10 pieces of penny candy! Trading thrown away garbage for candy is pretty awesome if you ask me! I can't bear to do the math on how much money I'd have now if I'd saved all those dimes over the years, along with the compound interest, but I'm sure it'd be a lot (we can always ask one of those people who somehow made it through many boring accounting classes to get their degree!). Instead, let's focus on the fact that the litter was being picked up and the roadsides were a little more beautiful, shall we? At least that's what I'm choosing to focus on here!

That love of natural spaces and my compulsion to fix and protect them (one might even say improve!) has followed me throughout my life. If I had to walk outside to get to a meeting in another building as part of one of my corporate jobs, I would stop and grab a plastic bottle in the street on my way.

I understand some people find picking up trash gross or too much trouble, but for me, I felt more ashamed and embarrassed if I *didn't* pick up the trash I saw. My conscience would bother me the rest of the day, so I quickly learned that I would have a much better day overall and way less guilt if I simply took the extra 2 seconds to bend over and grab the garbage on my way through. And I couldn't stop at picking up trash only while at work. It carried over into anywhere I was.

I love hiking! I especially love any hike that takes me beyond the crowds and into quieter, more secluded areas of wilderness. Of course, there are very few areas that are untouched by humans, so even in those areas, I often find trash (not always carelessly tossed – it can be blown in via storms and other means). Regardless of how it got there, I hike with a spare bag in my backpack to make it easy to grab trash along the trail and hike it out.

One of my WHYs for anything I do is to leave the planet better than I found it. This manifests itself in different ways in my personal life, but also in the work that I do.

As it became more and more clear that I needed to leave my good corporate job, I started paying attention to some of the things I didn't like. Now, to be fair and very transparent, I had a long list of things I did like about that job, which was one of the reasons that it was such a difficult decision to leave. However, as I thought about it, one of the things I strongly disliked was my commute. I was spending more than one and a half hours a day in the car. As a person who loves efficiency, this wasn't it! But what really bothered me was so much deeper than that.

I was struggling with the environmental impact of me driving a car for that length of time (mostly idling in stop-and-go traffic during peak travel hours). As someone who loves the natural world, the harm I was causing was inescapable. I had traveled to my corporate job on public transportation (shout out to my bus buddies!) for nearly a decade and had not minded the commute nearly as much, but with 2 young children and strict rules on what time I needed to pick them up from childcare, I eventually had had to make the choice to drive a personal vehicle instead.

When I started my coaching and speaking business, I knew that I wanted my work to align to my values and was intentional on building my business accordingly. WHERE I worked needed to support my WHY.

I've been deliberate on choosing work that doesn't require me to travel regularly, whether across town or across the country. I'm certain I would have different opportunities available to me if I would be willing to compromise on this. But here's something I know unequivocally: It wouldn't fit my definition of success because it doesn't support one my WHYs.

I am not willing to go back to a world of work misery, so I need to make choices that don't take me down that path. I feel far more successful knowing that my WHERE allows me to live out my WHY.

Let's look at another way that WHERE can support and advance your WHY.

One of the greatest problems we face if we want to continue to live on this planet (and I'm assuming you're reading this from Earth) is global warming. Remember that compulsion I have to protect and fix the planet? Well, for me, it stopped being enough to do my part and pick up trash and drive less. I needed to do more.

I did research and found a great organization doing great work in the climate crisis space. The Climate Reality Project (CRP) focuses on education to help everyone understand not just the grave challenges we're facing, but how they can start to make change happen. As someone who started a business to educate and empower people to take positive action, this was exactly the sort of organization I wanted to join!

As luck would have it, the very next training being offered by CRP would be in Minneapolis a few months after my research had led me to them. I applied to be part of their leadership corps and was accepted!

It's a wonderfully terrifying thing to see something you say you want actually come into being. Now that I was accepted, I needed to attend the leadership corps. I needed to the commit to three full days of training and do the corresponding work expected of a leader. I found myself wondering some version of, "What did I get myself into?" repeatedly in the weeks leading up to the training. It was also a good reminder for me on how fear can stop us, if we let it.

I was determined to follow through and I made my way to Minneapolis on a hot August afternoon. After some issues with hotel booking and finally finding a place to rest my head for the night, I was ready to begin training early the following morning.

I walked into the convention center and was completely and fully blown away. I was early (as I have a tendency to be when I'm nervous!) and had plenty of time to walk around and get the lay of the land. Most importantly, I found the coffee and grabbed a cup as I got settled. I was assigned a table and headed there to wait to meet everyone else as they arrived.

I met interesting people in every line of work imaginable from across the U.S. and across the world. I heard amazing speakers share topics not just on the global challenges, but on the specific impacts the climate crisis is having in the Midwest. This took a challenge at a planetary level and made it specific to WHERE we were in the world (and WHERE many of us at the training lived).

It was exactly the education I needed to help me make

global warming relevant for my family, friends, and neighbors. I needed to understand how the problems were manifesting themselves WHERE I was in order to be able to share that knowledge with others. I needed to ground all of my presentations and community education in the local knowledge of WHERE in order for it to have any resonance with the impacted systems globally.

What an awesome experience! It absolutely helped me advance my WHY, but it also immediately connected me to a community of WHOs that I would not have met in any other capacity.

Being in a room with more than 1,200 other people that cared the way I did was a powerful, life-changing experience. I'd spent my whole life feeling alone, but I wasn't. We'd been there all along, whether we knew each other or not. It gave me the courage and the support I needed to take my educational experience and leadership training back out into the world, using my WHY to spur me on. More importantly, it helped me build relationships WHERE I needed them most: close to home.

If your WHY is to become the absolute best at the thing you're great at, your WHERE must be where the top people in your industry are. If I want to be the best financial analyst on Wall Street, the best place for me to make that happen is, you guessed it, working for a firm on Wall Street. A small-sized financial services company in the Midwest is not going to be nearly as helpful for me. Can it still be done? You bet. Ask the Oracle of Omaha, Warren Buffet. But by and large, being where the action is on Wall Street will propel you further and faster than other routes.

If your WHY is to create equality in tech, you need to

be in places WHERE lots of technology work is going on so you can have an impact.

If your WHY is your children, your WHERE needs to reflect that through being close enough to home that you can spend as much time with your kids as possible.

Whatever your WHY, you will advance it further with WHERE.

10

WHEN?

"*Life, as it is called, is for most of us one long postponement.*"
— Henry Miller

YESTERDAY

Let's say you manage to find the right place, whether strategically or by accident. That will absolutely help you be successful. But you know what will supercharge it? Being in the right place at the exact right time!

Can we be strategic about it? Not always. Surprises and shifts happen that most experts miss predicting (remember the 2008 housing market crash?). No one gets it right all the time. That's life. But it's always the right time to create opportunity for ourselves.

As I mentioned, I graduated from college with a degree in computers in May of 2000. All of my friends in the degree program that graduated in the quarters prior to when

I did were in high demand. You see, they'd all taken at least a few classes in the programming language COBOL as part of our degree program.

Most financial institutions had (and some still have) mainframe computers to run their daily operations. That includes important things like financial transactions and money movement. In order to save space, (which at one time cost a premium, unlike me getting a terabyte of storage "free" with a year's subscription to Microsoft Office now) programmers shortened the year portion of the date from 4 characters to 2 characters, using 96 instead of 1996 as an example.

This worked out pretty well until we neared the end of the 20th century. And then it was discovered that a year of 00 could be interpreted as 1900 or 2000 any other year ending in 00, which could significantly impact all sorts of things, including financial transactions. The discovery was officially dubbed the Y2K crisis.

Let's go back to my college campus in 1999, where I'm sure a Dave Matthews Band CD was playing on repeat...

As I mentioned, all my friends that graduated before I did were in demand because of their skillset. Companies desperately needed anyone that knew how to program in COBOL and were hiring anyone with a pulse to work on the Y2K problem.

As benign as it sounds now, at the time, we didn't know if we'd have electricity or groceries, let alone banks and money and all sorts of other things. The worst-case scenario was a full shut-down of pretty much everything. Therefore, most companies had a lot riding on fixing the year glitch before the ball dropped on New Year's Eve.

I knew plenty of entry-level programmers who got very lucrative work straight out of college simply because of WHEN they were graduating with an in-demand skillset. Unfortunately for me, I wasn't one of them.

All was not lost though. After the clock struck midnight and we ushered in a new century complete with power and food and flush toilets (and a whole lot of the song 1999 by Prince), technology was hailed not as a threat, but as a savior! Better still, companies were ready to invest in new technology after throwing so much money at their older tech investments as we entered the internet age.

With that timing, I had my choice of several job offers to do web development after graduation. Graduating from college and getting a "good job" was about to be checked off the checklist! Yahoo (the exclamation, not the internet company that was the go-to search instead of Google at the time, unless of course you were using Ask Jeeves…)!

Had I been strategically planning for this exact moment in time? Nope. It was a collection of events and circumstances that led me there, including narrowly escaping a fate worse than death when I clawed out of the evil clutches of the accounting program.

But WHEN I graduated absolutely impacted my career in positive and negative ways. I missed that whole get-rich-before-Y2K thing. I caught the web developer wave. Of course, the internet bubble burst a few years later and I needed to adjust and find another job. These types of WHENs ebb and flow over the course of the career. Sometimes you catch the wave; sometimes you swim like the dickens to not get pulled under as it crashes on your head.

TODAY

Does WHEN always have to be an unknown timeframe where we simply hope everything works out in our favor? Absolutely not. There are plenty of WHENs we can control.

Let's take an example we all daydream about regularly: getting a raise.

Of course, we'd all like to get paid more for doing less work. And many of us would be glad to at least get paid more for doing the same or slightly more work. If I work for an organization and I want to ask for a raise, I need to have some reasons why I deserve it. And it can't be just because Barry in Accounting makes more than me (aw nuts, I should have stuck with accounting as my major!).

I need to be able to describe the value I bring to the organization. I need to share the outcomes and results I've delivered. I probably need to remind my boss of all the things I've worked on recently, since she has way too much to do and likely doesn't remember it all.

If all I've got to go on is that Barry makes more, there's no point in asking for a raise.

Think about it. If the roles were reversed and you were the boss, would that be compelling evidence for you to give out more cash to an employee? No way! That argument is weak at best and pathetic at worst.

But even if my story is solid and I've got demonstrated results, metrics, and even awards to prove it, WHEN will be a factor in my request for a raise.

If the organization I work for is on an annual performance cycle, I can't wait until after that cycle has started to begin to tell my story. It's too late. The processes that most large organization use when assessing performance annually are too burdensome to allow for late additions of information. What usually ends up happening is that data is dismissed or deferred for the following year, even if a person has done a rockstar job. I need to be telling my story early and often so that my boss can advocate on my behalf.

And speaking of my boss, I can't ask her about giving me a raise in a week where there have been budget cuts announced and she's been in back-to-back meetings for days and now she's walking to her car trying to get to an after-work event that she's already late for. She won't be able to hear me. She won't be willing to consider it. She'll be thinking about that after-work event and what excuse she is going to give for being late (possibly her idiot employee begging for a raise at the wrong time on the wrong day!). I need to make sure that the person or people I share my value with not only understand it, but believe it and are ready to do what it takes to get that raise (if they don't have the authority to grant it themselves). My story of WHAT I do and HOW I do it also needs to align with WHEN I share that story.

WHEN matters.

SOMEDAY

Time flies whether we're having fun or not, doesn't it? I am often astounded how quickly a week, month, quarter, or year can fly by. Many of my coaching clients are shocked to discover that they've spent far longer (usually years more) in a job that didn't suit them or they despised. And yet, because time flies and we fill it with seemingly urgent tasks, it's not uncommon to wake up one day and wonder how you managed for so long.

Sidebar: I'm clearly not talking about the year 2020. That has had a unique timeline all its own.

If time flies, then we need to be especially vigilant of our WHEN if we want any control or say in the matter. We need to consciously be choosing WHEN as a means to check in with ourselves. If we don't, the greatest enemy to WHEN will emerge:

Someday.

Someday is a fantasy world that we wish existed; it's not a real place. And it most certainly is NOT an actual time. It has nothing to do with WHEN, other than to prevent us from ever getting around to something. We all battle someday as we go through our days. Often, someday wins the daily match-up. It sounds a lot like this:

When will I go through that box of old stuff my parents gave me? Someday.

When will I volunteer at a charity doing work that is important to me? Someday (usually in another equally magical world where you have "free time").

When will I carve out time for myself to do that really fun thing I love? Someday.

When will I spend more time with my friends and family? The delightful combo answer of Someday + Free Time.

If someday is so terrible, why do we let it hang around and derail our WHEN?

Sometimes it's the little annoyances we simply don't want to deal with. When will I go through that pile of junk mail on the counter? Not today, since I just added 3 more things to the stack! Going through it now would take even longer than it would have before I checked the mail. I'll do it someday, you know, when I have more free time!

Sometimes it's something we want to do but feel guilty taking that time for ourselves. When will I complete that professional development class that I know will help me in my career? These sorts of things often get pushed back to someday because of the urgent thing your boss's boss needs this week. For anyone that has lived the cycle of pushing off things because "work is just too busy right now", I want you to hear this public service announcement loud and clear. Work will ALWAYS be busy. There will ALWAYS be too much to do. Stop deferring your interests, your life, and your dreams for an organization that won't even bother to get you a card when you leave it.

Sometimes it's the necessary and potentially life-altering things. When will I schedule that appointment with the doctor for the screening test that a person my age should have? This becomes far more urgent and important when the lump or bump or abnormal test result indicates that our someday should have been sooner.

We all have things that we defer for another time (trust me, I'm a pro! If you'd like, I can list all the ways that procrastination pays off. Not right now obviously. Someday...).

Sometimes, we believe we are doing this in the interest of prioritization and keen time management. More often though, we do this because of fear.

Since someday is a fantasy world that doesn't actually exist, let's invent another fantasy world to be its opposite.

Let's create a world where a team of awesome people just like yourself showed up one night and took care of everything on your someday list from sending a thank-you note to your mother-in-law for your birthday gift, to getting the house repainted, to booking that dream vacation to Alaska.

When you wake up, every possible thing that you were going to do someday is now done. Hooray for you! Only one question: What will you do today now that everything is taken care of?

This is where the fear lives. If we have no excuses or reasons why we're so busy, we might actually need to spend time where we're fully present with our family and friends. We might actually have to get involved with that charity doing great work. We might actually have to take the leap and make progress toward a secret (or not-so-secret!) dream. There is nothing standing in our way. And that can be absolutely and completely terrifying.

The writer Sarah Ban Breathnach said it best, "Many of us have unconsciously erected seemingly insurmountable barriers to protect ourselves from failing or succeeding." (Ban Breathnach 1995)

Having the ability to enjoy friends, or life, or help others, or chase down a dream are things that are scary because we might actually be successful at them. It's hard to imagine a world where we're doing exactly what we want and loving every minute of it. So, we let someday be the crutch we lean on to keep us from getting there.

Well that sucks. I hate it when reality slaps me in the face, don't you?

Don't go giving up now! Here's what we do.

We do both. In the same way that Someday doesn't

exist, neither does Everything's-Done-Land (worst theme park of all time, BTW). When you're fighting an imaginary enemy, all it takes is a little imagination to outsmart it regularly.

So, we chip away at those things that are most important to us. Want to write a book? Sit down and write a sentence. Want to volunteer? Find a half hour to head to an organization and lend a hand. Want to spend more time with friends and family? Call someone right now to see how they're doing.

We can overcome someday through small actions toward what matters most. And if you never get around to going through that box from your parents, so what?

WHO? PART 2

"At times, our own light goes out and is rekindled by a spark from another person. Each of us has cause to think with deep gratitude of those who have lighted the flame within us."
– Albert Schweitzer

RELATIONSHIPS REALLY DO MATTER

Did you notice that in all 6 W's, there were stories about people? Go ahead, flip back through. I'll wait.

This would actually be a pretty boring (and short!) book if there were no people involved. Can you imagine spending time reading and attempting to learn anything without the WHO piece? It'd be a snooze-fest! We're talking super-thick-20-pound-college-textbook-you-spent-$300-on-and-never-opened boring (thanks for that, professor of my intro to business law class, by the way!).

The implication is there's more to the WHO piece than first meets the eye.

We absolutely rely on WHO we know as we are building our version of success. WHO is important over the meandering course of our careers as we gain new skills, try new things, seek out meaning, and do our best to set ourselves up for success authentically. But that's not the end of WHO in the formula.

WHO is absolutely additive. As you grow your network of colleagues, friends, and known associates, your options for the present and future continue expand. However, as we've seen throughout our exploration of the other 5 W's, WHO is at play in each of them as well. WHO becomes a multiplier across the entire formula (when used effectively!) to transform your level of success.

We need to remember this and revise the formula accordingly:

((Who + What) * How * Why * (Where + When)) * **Who**

WHO has become not only an element of the formula, but also the thing that supercharges every element of the formula for maximum success and enjoyment. People matter. Relationships matter. They are not to be used as a way to get you where you want to go in your career or life; they are powerful to your success because you can't succeed alone. Want more excitement, purpose, and joy at work? Invest your time in people.

DEATH AND TAXES

Let's get real and talk about something we all know is coming, though most of us are fuzzy on the WHEN: Death. The WHEN for taxes is much more regular and basically guarantees job security for all those accountants until they hit the other eventuality!

Although death is coming for all of us, it's neither the most pleasant thought nor is it a great conversation starter at parties. But it does help us to see the power of WHO in a different light.

People on their deathbed are frequently described as being surrounded by loved ones. That's the way most people want to leave the world, if given a choice, in close proximity with their family and friends.

As David Whyte so eloquently explains, *"Death is not impressed by what we have done, unless what we have done leaves a legacy of life... What is remembered in all our work is what is still alive in the hearts and minds of others."* (Whyte 2001)

Very few people express regret about not working enough hours or inventing the perfect approach to manage projects. When the time comes, most people wish they had more time with those they know and love.

To paraphrase one of my favorite Christmas movies of all time (not *Die Hard*, though that one is great in different ways!), *Love Actually*: None of the messages from the people on board the planes headed for the Twin Towers were of hate, they were all of love.

It's a version of the same deathbed wisdom that we come across so often in our lives that we start to ignore it.

Or maybe it's the discomfort we all feel when confronted with our own mortality that keeps us from taking action on that knowledge. Talk about awkward!

But there is great value to be had in recognizing that WHO plays a bigger role in our lives than we usually let on. Especially in the workplace where for many of us, we feel like we have to keep our professional lives separate from our personal lives as if the person we are when we stroll through the doors of an organization is somehow different than the person we are when we stroll through the doors of our home.

Sidebar: I know that there are many workplaces that prevent or forbid people to bring their authentic selves into the workplace. As much as I want that not to be the case, it's reality for many groups of people, including LGBTQIA+, BIPOC, and women. The point here is that we are the same person, with or without the mask we feel like we need to wear, and the relationships we develop at work, at home, and in the world matter greatly. End sidebar.

WHO has an impact across all 6 W's. If it takes a village to raise a child, it takes an even bigger village to help that human grow into the best, most successful version of themselves over the course of their lifetime. I know that's not likely to fit on a bumper sticker, but you get the idea.

We can get so caught up in WHAT we do that we have no time left for WHO and this is often where our definitions of success get tangled up. We lose sight of the most critical piece.

The relationships we build over a lifetime of work and life, love and loss are more powerful and more important than we often give them credit. These relationships have the power to transform our work into a masterpiece. They can transform our lives into well-lived experiences. They can transform our world into a better place for everyone and everything in it. Relationships are transformational if we let them become so.

Your success is forever bound to others. The sooner we acknowledge that fact, the sooner we can get on with transforming ourselves, our work and lives, and the world.

12

PUTTING IT ALL TOGETHER

"What if the world is holding its breath – waiting for you to take the place that only you can fill?"
— David Whyte

Daniel Eugene "Rudy" Ruettiger was not expected to be a famous college football player. He wasn't a great athlete. He was an even worse student. And yet, he inspired the film (Rudy 1993), along with countless individuals who hear him share his story of perseverance and unwavering belief in a dream.

Here's the backstory. Rudy grew up watching Notre Dame football with his family. Though the odds were infinitesimally small, he wanted to play football at the university he'd watched on TV as a child. Rudy didn't have the grades in high school to be accepted into most colleges, but especially not a prestigious school like Notre Dame.

After high school, Rudy went to work at a steel mill where several of his family and friends worked. It was a good, stable job, but Rudy wanted more. He saved his money for tuition at Notre Dame. He finally got the courage to take a shot at his dream after his best friend was killed in an accident at work.

Rudy arrived at the Notre Dame campus after his friend's funeral, but because it was after standard hours, the only person available to talk to was a priest. The priest listened to Rudy's story and his big dream. Although the priest couldn't help him get into Notre Dame, the priest did offer to reach out to one of his contacts at a local community college. He told Rudy that if he could get good grades for a semester, he could try applying to Notre Dame. It all came down to WHO Rudy knew. It gave him a slight edge to be accepted at community college where he might not otherwise have been accepted. He then needed to put in the work to become the academic he hadn't managed to be during high school.

It wasn't a straight shot to his dream of playing football. There was a pretty good chance it wouldn't work out. The only reason I'm re-telling this story today though, is because it did turn out. None of us would have ever heard of Rudy Ruettiger if it hadn't.

So, Rudy had to study and get good grades. He worked and scrimped and saved to continue going to school. He applied every semester to Notre Dame. On his last semester of junior year, he was finally accepted. But it wasn't enough to be accepted to his dream university. As soon as he was accepted to Notre Dame, he tried out for the football team as a walk-on. He was an unlikely choice for even the practice team, but the coaches saw the fire in his eyes and couldn't deny that he was more enthusiastic than anyone else on the field.

Most good managers, like good coaches, will hire for passion. It's easy to teach a new skillset, but almost impossible to teach someone how to care about something they don't. I would gladly take a team of Rudy's to try to accomplish any goal over a team of highly skilled but disengaged people. They knew they could train Rudy to the WHAT as long as he kept bringing his energy to practice.

Rudy basically had to agree to be a live practice dummy; he was beat up, knocked down, and pushed around at every practice. But he was living his dream! No one says the dream will be glamourous. In fact, it's usually the opposite. You have to be willing to deal with the awful stuff as much as any good when you pursue a dream. That's what makes your WHY so critical. Without a compelling WHY, you'll be like all the other reasonable people who give up on the dream when it gets hard.

I don't know Rudy's WHY. In fact, I can't begin to guess what would compel any human to stand still while 11 of the biggest people on the planet hurl themselves at you full force with the single goal of knocking you to the ground so they can take a strangely shaped orb down a field. Here's what I do know. His WHY was powerful enough for him to do it. And to do it repeatedly in every practice for 2 years, without any real hope of getting into an actual game.

HOW did he do it? With an indefatigable will and a higher than average amount of perseverance, he kept doing what he needed to do. Not because the odds got better over time, simply because his WHY compelled him forward while his HOW made his approach the gold standard at practices. He had heart. He didn't give up, even when everyone said he should. He kept going.

Was Rudy in the right place at the right time? It sure seems like it. He'd tried and failed to get accepted to Notre Dame many times before he was finally admitted. His dogged persistence before and during try-outs allowed him to make an impression on the football coaching staff. WHERE and WHEN definitely helped him.

For Rudy, his HOW and WHY were so much bigger than his other 4 W's. He needed the other four to make it happen, but the HOW and WHY multiplied it in a way that took a small amount of athletic ability and allowed him to play college football on one of the best teams in the nation at that time.

The entire film of Rudy's story is filled with WHO part 2 moments. It's the teacher that discourages Rudy from following his dream. It's the parent that tries to let him down easy rather than see his heart broken if the dream doesn't happen. It's the leader of the Notre Dame athletic boosters that bars him from participating. But it's also the chance meeting with the priest that gets him a start at a community college. It's the teacher's assistant that tutors and befriends him. It's the groundskeeper of the football field that gives him a job and a place to stay. It's the football team that rallies around him when he needs it most.

In our family, we watch the movie Rudy every fall. It's a beautiful reminder of the power of perseverance and that every once in a while, the underdog emerges as the champion. Even now when I hear the strains of the triumphant music that is playing when he takes the field, my heart leaps for joy and a single, happy tear streams down my cheek (so that last part is a bit too movie-ending perfect, but it'd be cool if that happened as the credits rolled on this, right?!?).

The Success Authentically formula on its own does absolutely nothing for you. It's literally just words on a page.

The power comes from you taking the time to answer these questions for yourself and to put them into action. Don't you want to find the excitement, purpose, and joy that is out there waiting for you?

Will you be the person that turns this knowledge into positive action?

What are you waiting for?

THANK YOU AND FREE GIFT

Thank you for reading! I hope you found this helpful and took positive action by incorporating the strategies discussed to unlock excitement, purpose, and joy at work! If you enjoyed this book, please consider leaving a five-star review. You can use this link:

WorkAuthentically.com/ReviewSuccessAuthentically

I know you're busy and I genuinely appreciate your time. Your review can help others find this book, in addition to supporting me.

I know all too well it's not easy to find success authentically, so to help you on your journey I've got a FREE GIFT for you. Go to WorkAuthentically.com/Resources get exclusive career insights and inspiration delivered to your inbox weekly.

Authentically yours,
    Ally

ACKNOWLEDGMENTS

Thank you to the **Great Creator**. This book came through me, not from me. I have done my best to preserve it. Chalk up any errors to my humanness, which I celebrate in all its imperfection.

Thank you to **Aaron**, who is least likely to read this far. But that's because you're busy doing all the things I'm not so I can write a book! You're a true partner and all I need in this life. I love you.

Thank you to **Heather** for always being there. You are an unequivocal success in all the ways that matter.

Thank you to my BFF **Bruce**. I never fully understood your compulsion for writing. Until now. And there is no going back! You remind me to do good work whenever I lose my bearings. The first 97% is easy… the last 3% is the work of a lifetime!

Thank you to my **Interrupting Cows**! You motivate me to keep improving. You are the best and most effective hands-on leadership course I've ever experienced! I love you moo-moos!

Thank you to my **Launch Team!** I so appreciate you choosing to share a little of your most precious resource, time, with me. I will gladly return the favor when you want to release a book, chat for hours, launch a product, or have a brainstorming session. But I'm not available the day you're moving and can't help you carry anything. Sorry.

Thank you to the **many amazing people** I've had the privilege of working with up to this point. Some were specifically named in this book - many more are unnamed (they have lovely names, though!). I am forever indebted for their lessons taught, wisdom shared, and memories made. As I thought about the ways the formula has manifested in my life, I got to travel through my past and revisit jobs and teams that were truly a joy for me. I'm beyond grateful that I've had awesome career experiences as it helped me recognize those times when I wasn't in one.

And finally, thank **YOU** for reading. Thank you for daring to believe work doesn't have to be a steaming pile of misery. I wish you excitement, purpose, and joy on your quest for success authentically.

ABOUT THE AUTHOR

Ally Bubb spent her entire childhood and adult life with absolutely no answer to the awkward question of *"What do you want to be when you grow up?"* Now, she uses her superpowers to ask better career questions and help others do the same. Ally combines enthusiasm, honesty, and authenticity into her work as a career coach and speaker, teaching people to tell compelling career stories and take positive action because when people genuinely love what they do, our workplaces, homes, and world are transformed.

Work Authentically is reinventing the world of work by teaching people to leverage their unique style, approach, and way of being through presentations, workshops, and individual and group coaching. Sign up for our free weekly newsletter at WorkAuthentically.com.

You can follow Work Authentically on LinkedIn, Twitter, and Instagram.

BOOKS BY ALLY BUBB

Change Authentically: A Guide to Transform Your Job and Life Through Positive Action

You Got This!: Move Beyond Fear to Make Change Happen!

Get Out of Your Pajamas, Take a Shower, and Talk to Someone: Job Searching During a Pandemic, Economic Downturn, Recession, or Other Crisis

Made in the USA
Monee, IL
11 January 2021